"A supportive, sensitive guide to ancestor work, *The Magic in Your Genes* will help you unlock powers you've had access to all along, nestled deep within. Your DNA is an infinite record of ancestral memory; and genealogist, nurse, and priestess Cairelle Crow walks you through the basics of DNA, how to navigate a genealogical report, and the spiritual practice of ancestral healing."

—**Benebell Wen,** author of *The Tao of Craft* and *Holistic Tarot*

"Cairelle Crow has gifted the world with a treasure—a book that successfully weaves the delicate threads of genealogy and magic. Crow guides readers on a journey of self-discovery that is at once healing and empowering. Many of us have wondered about those who came before us and wished we had ways to connect with them. Thankfully, there's no longer a need to wonder or wish: Crow provides the tools to chart your lineage and awaken the magic in your DNA. Blending science with spellcraft, this book leads readers to the sacred crossroads where past and present, spirit and identity intersect."

—**Antonio Pagliarulo,** author of *The Evil Eye*

"In my opinion, there is no one form of trauma healing more important than healing the cross-generational ancestral imprints that are in our blood. As my mother said, 'No one heals 'til the ghosts speak.' *The Magic in Your Genes*, this well-written and astutely relevant book, adds refined insights and effective healing tools to this work. Bravo to Cairelle Crow for a book whose healing hand will indeed be felt by generations past, currently living, and those to come."

—**Orion Foxwood,** author of *Mountain Conjure and Southern Root Work* and *The Tree of Enchantment*

"Cairelle Crow's *The Magic in Your Genes* is a heart-opening, down-to-earth, and completely enchanting journey into genealogy, inheritance, ancestral work, and rituals. She has written a book that is inclusive of many communities, encourages the reader to follow their truth, and will surprise you, even if you are an old hand at this topic. Cairelle is gracious and shares her personal, sometimes difficult, experiences to ground this work and to offer examples that make it concrete for the reader. This book is unique, and I believe it will be seen as the start of a new approach to ancestral work."

—**Ivo Dominguez Jr.,** author of *Four Elements of the Wise*

"Cairelle Crow weaves together the science of genealogy and the magic of honoring the ancestors in her wonderful book, *The Magic in Your Genes*. In this book, we learn simple yet powerful techniques to help us step into the world of our beloved dead as we unravel the mystery of our own DNA. Crow masterfully simplifies complex genetic science so that we may delve deeply into where we come from and connect to our ancestors on a profound spiritual level."

—**Chris Allaun,** author of *A Guide of Spirits*

"Cairelle Crow has crafted a fascinating read into the world of genealogical research. This book is filled with science and magic that balance and support the daunting research of one's family tree."

—**Najah Lightfoot,** author of *Good Juju* **and** *Powerful Juju*

"In *The Magic in Your Genes*, Cairelle Crow has written an intellectual, deeply compassionate, and forward-thinking book. Filled with enough science to appeal to the scholar and enough magic to appeal to those who practice, this book is a must-read for anyone interested in genealogy work, whether for their own purposes or as a career."

—**Christine Cunningham Ashworth,** author of *Scott Cunningham—The Path Taken*

"*The Magic in Your Genes* is beautifully written for all people who are ready to begin the quest of searching out their roots and creating a family tree. As you follow the carefully articulated steps, you will find genealogy understandable, even for the novice. Cairelle Crow demonstrates that genealogy is a magical tool that everyone can use to write their unique story. This is a book you can return to again and again on your path of discovery."

—**Laura Louella,** author and editor of *Brigid's Light*

"Cairelle Crow's *The Magic in Your Genes* offers beautiful, smart, and divine ways to combine genealogy and spiritual practice that not only helped me to connect with my living ancestry but reminded me of my own destiny of becoming an ancestor. Whether you are working with blood ancestors or spiritual lineages, this book offers powerful and illuminating methods and rituals that will become mainstays of ancestral honoring in years to come."

—**Priestess Brandi Auset,** author of *The Goddess Guide*

"Whether you are new to genealogy and ancestral work or have been immersed in your family's history for decades, all seekers will benefit from the inclusivity, magical wisdom, and exhaustive research found in *The Magic in Your Genes*. Cairelle Crow does an excellent job of breaking down the science and biology without losing the magic of the journey or the wonder of tracing your family tree.

"I will be rereading *The Magic in Your Genes* on my walk with the ancestors many times, learning something new each time."

—**Jamie Della,** author of *The Book of Spells*

"Knowing where we come from informs who we are, and *The Magic in Your Genes* informs us in powerful, magickal, and practical ways. Cairelle Crow brings traditional genealogy firmly into the realm of Ancestor Magick with opportunities to creatively explore our generational and spiritual lineages, as well as approaches for deep healing and inclusivity. *The Magic in Your Genes* will be a mainstay in book collections and expand our current concepts of ancestral honoring and ritual."

—**Kimberly Moore,** founder and priestess of MotherHouse of the Goddess

The MAGIC in Your Genes

Your Personal Path to
ANCESTOR WORK

CAIRELLE CROW

WEISER BOOKS

This edition first published in 2023 by Weiser Books, an imprint of
Red Wheel/Weiser, LLC
with offices at:
65 Parker Street, Suite 7
Newburyport, MA 01950
www.redwheelweiser.com

ISBN: 978-1-57863-776-8

Library of Congress Cataloging-in-Publication Data

Names: Crow, Cairelle, 1967- author.
Title: The magic in your genes : your personal path to ancestor work (bringing together the science of DNA
with the timeless power of ritual and spellcraft) / Cairelle Crow.
Description: Newburyport, MA : Weiser Books, 2023. | Includes bibliographical references. | Summary:
"Have you been searching for a way to find deeper connection with your ancestors? Or would you like to
learn how to reach your spirit guides? This book offers a route to becoming more in tune with your personal
genealogical background so that you can begin to understand more about your ancestors. It has a primer
on the basics of DNA and genetic genealogy practices, so no prior knowledge is required to put the book to
use. Magical tips and techniques are placed throughout to help the reader utilize both technical and magical
resources as appropriate to the content in each chapter. It is geared to those with a known recent genealogical
history (parents, grandparents) but is also appropriate for those who are adopted or who have other situations, such as a misattributed parentage event"-- Provided by publisher.
Identifiers: LCCN 2022056508 | ISBN 9781578637768 (trade paperback) | ISBN 9781633412606
(kindle edition)
Subjects: LCSH: Genetic genealogy--Popular works. | Genetic genealogy--Religious aspects. | Ancestral
shrines. | Ancestral worship. | Witchcraft. | Witches. | BISAC: BODY, MIND & SPIRIT / Witchcraft (see
 also RELIGION / Wicca) | BODY, MIND & SPIRIT / Magick Studies Classification: LCC CS21.3
.C76 2023 | DDC 929.1072--dc23/eng/20230103
LC record available at https://lccn.loc.gov/2022056508

Cover art "Mother Eve" (2013) © Ramy Tadros. Used by permission of Artmajeur.

The shared cM Project chart courtesy of DNA Painter.
Flow/tree/chart graphics by Marisa McCall.
Toolbox icon by Cairelle Crow.
Interior by Steve Amarillo / Urban Design LLC
Typeset in Orpheus and Adobe Garamond

Printed in the United States of America
IBI
10 9 8 7 6 5 4 3 2 1

For Silas and Judah, whose bright smiles and open hearts bless me with gratitude for the past and hope for the future; and for Hyndla, ancient hag, völva, giantess, cave dweller, wolf rider, guardian of bloodlines, keeper of names, astral walker of the weft and warp, who shines just enough light so that those who seek truths with good intent might find them.

Contents

Introduction

Right here, right now? This is precious. This is life. You're alive. Somehow,
all of the genetic material of all those thousands of ancestors came
together in the perfect combination to make you, exactly as you are.
That's magical—it's the greatest kind of magic I know. Our very existence.

—Loretta Lost, *The Fireproof Girl*

Genealogy is magical. Within it lies the opportunity to engage in research that results in the potential discovery of an interrelatedness with all the peoples of the world, and to gain a feeling of profound connection to the constellation of humanity. There is room for everyone on this path of magic. Envision a beautiful tree fluttering with the leafy papers of lives lived, births and deaths, arrivals and departures, connections, news and stories, roots buried deep in the earth in which the tree stands, much as we stand now on the shoulders of our ancestors. As it is with trees in nature, so it is in genealogy that each tree must have the proper resources to grow to its fullest potential. For many hundreds of years, people have written down family histories and lineages and kept records that allow us now to glean bits of information through diligent investigation of those historical documents. Despite the near-endless variety of people researching their ancestral roots, every person's tree has one thing in common: there is a precise order in which our genealogical ancestors and their branches are arranged. For a lucky few, traditional "paper" genealogy research yields many branches filled with ancestral leaves that are brimming with vestiges of lives past. For most others, several or more branches are less obvious, the leaves sparse, and the work of discovery is challenging. Some, whether through adoption or another circumstance that has rendered their branches invisible or inaccessible, see only themselves, and their ancestral explorations are extremely difficult or even impossible with traditional methods.

Genetic genealogy has changed the way many genealogists approach their research, and, thankfully, direct-to-consumer genealogical DNA testing has now leveled the field and even the most difficult mysteries can usually be solved. Every one of us—those with ample family history resources, those with none, and all in between—can send in a saliva sample with the expectation that results will grant the knowledge needed to create and grow an accurate genealogical family tree based on truth and facts. Magical, indeed! I believe it is vitally important for each one of us to do genealogical DNA testing, to accurately document our genealogical, genetic, and chosen ancestral lines to the best of our ability, and to follow the most current ethics, guidelines, and standards to build a family story that is based on truth. One day a descendant (and by this I don't just mean genetic offspring!) will look at your tree and they'll be so thankful for the chance to get to know you long after you're gone, much as we look now to discover the stories of our own ancestors.

For those of us who walk the razor's edge between the evidence-based nature of genealogy and the intangible, magical essence of our own sacred divine, the blending of traditional and genetic genealogical research with our own spiritual and creative preferences occurs naturally as we do the work of searching for ancestral kindred. Genealogy and magic, while vastly different, do not have to be mutually exclusive. The combination of the two is unbelievably powerful and manifests a connection that is breathtaking and life changing. Using personal magic opens a door that is not accessible otherwise and the view through it is extraordinary. You will see familiar faces that have shaped your idea of yourself as a magical person and you will encounter new faces that will open unexpected paths and round out your magical practice in a profound way.

Sometimes events have transpired that make traditional genealogy research difficult or undesirable. The most common that I've encountered over many years of genealogy work is adoption. The second is the discovery that a parent (usually a father) is not the genetic parent. One of the effects of collective trauma on groups of people is having to do genealogy research within the confines of nonexistent, altered, or destroyed documentation of ancestors. There is also a misconception that the pursuit of biological, genetic-based genealogy is the only way to do genealogy work. This is not so. There are countless people who have chosen to remove themselves from the harmful or hurtful (or both) ramifications of a toxic biological family, or who may have been expelled from one for any number of reasons, who have created a beautiful family woven together with the bonds of acceptance and love. There are also those who feel very connected to the family into which they were brought by way of adoption or another situation, and they don't wish to pursue a genetic angle to their genealogy. We get our personal power from many places, and the genealogical family of origin is only one source. Genealogy is the kind of magic that offers something for every scenario, and we each get to choose how we want to approach it. Every perspective, when researched well and documented properly, is valid.

It is my sincere belief that everyone, especially those who do their genealogy work strictly outside the genealogical family, should also consider doing work within the realm of ancestral healing. I assure you that does not mean that you must make space in your head for those who've hurt you, it doesn't mean forgiveness, or acceptance of bad behavior. You don't have to talk with anyone or open yourself up to further discomfort. You don't have to dismiss those in your life to whom you are close, be they genealogical or chosen family. What it does mean, in every scenario, is that there are ways to reach past the living, to travel to the land of the ancestors, to find connection to ancestral roots that go beyond the current incarnation of hurt and pain. You can walk a path of pride in your heritage while simultaneously living within your own boundaries as you do the hard work of healing. When you find a path to healing, you adjust your lineage permanently and this has a positive effect on future generations. It's important work, even for those who do not have genetic offspring and, instead, will one day become ancestors of influence.

A big dilemma I encountered while writing this book was how to best use pronouns, X- and Y-DNA descriptors, the words she, he, female, and male as they relate to biology and people, standard genealogy terms like maternal, paternal, mother, and father, and the words woman and man, while also being inclusive. For any genealogist, it is essential to be clear and consistent with the use of standardized phrases, wording, definitions, terms, explanations, and references so that the science that underlies genealogy can be easily understood as it is presented in currently available educational and other materials. It is also my heartfelt belief that genealogy is amorphous, like an ocean mist at the seashore, and it covers every person with a blanket of acceptance. No matter how we identify, or how the circumstances of our birth are defined, we each have unique family stories that are worthy of research and discovery. Genealogy is open to all races, ethnicities, genders, sexes, sexual preferences, religious and spiritual beliefs, physical and mental abilities, circumstances of birth, and beyond. Genealogy magic is for everyone.

In that mindset, then, I decided to reach out for help and clarification with my writing. I spoke with magical people within the LGBTQIA+ community, adult adoptees, those descended from enslaved persons, and others who feel disenfranchised and believe there is no room for them within the framework of genealogy. I asked questions, was corrected as needed (gently, thank you) regarding my own misunderstandings and misconceptions, and subsequently made changes in my writing. While I worked hard to find a balance, to share a variety of stories and scenarios, and to write in a way that I hope is more inclusive, I am also sure that the wording still isn't perfect and will not suit each person's individual lived reality.

In my experience, most, if not all, books on genealogy use hetero- and cis-focused language. It's the way people historically have been taught, and it's how many relate to the overall concepts. However, genealogy is always in flux. Leaders within the genealogy community are working hard to evolve old and tired concepts, and changes are actively taking place that ultimately will achieve the result that each person who works in genealogy's realm will feel their place in this world of documenting humanity is rooted within their own lived experience. It is a process, of course, and there is a long way to go. It is my sincerest hope, however, that those who have felt marginalized in the past will see the efforts being made by so many and will feel valued and part of a community that is meant to include us all. It is true that science can sometimes feel unassailable. It's also essential to remember that, while our chromosomes may categorize us to some extent, they do not rigidly define us. Humanity exists on a glorious spectrum, and we define ourselves. As you read this book, please know that every noun, pronoun, and adjective was written with the thought that there is more than one way to apply it, or not apply it, and I encourage you to mentally rearrange what needs moving so that the words reflect the truth of your individual story.

To give you a taste of the struggles and successes that are possible within the realm of genealogy magic, I have included my DNA adventures, examples of client research challenges and results, and snippets of stories shared by beloveds from the magical community. Except for my own immediate family, names have been changed, or are not mentioned, for privacy. I have also included information on DNA basics, testing and results, research, and documentation that should allow you to gain enough of an understanding to do entry level work on your own DNA testing results and family tree. However, in order to increase your scope beyond the most basic entry level, you will need to actively seek out other learning opportunities to further your knowledge and ensure you're making the most of all the information and tools that are available. Don't feel like you need an advanced degree, or that you need to pay a lot of money, to do genealogy work. For starters, the library is an excellent resource for genealogy books, and the librarians offer a wealth of knowledge as well. There are also plenty of groups online that offer mentoring and help with problem-solving, and hundreds of classes that go into more detail about a variety of topics within genealogy. Many of them are low-cost or free!

I believe that magic is the icing on the cake of genealogy, as it allows us to apply the energetic parts of ourselves to our work, and it opens a cosmic connection to those from whom we descend. However, the more traditional aspects of genealogy methodology must serve as the foundation so that we have a practical way to apply our knowledge, document our stories, and leave behind our legacy for those who will be arriving in our world at some point in the near or far future. As you look for and connect with those who have come and gone, I encourage you to use your words, your creativity, and your magic to tell your stories. Take the magical suggestions within these pages and make them your own. Reach deep within and trust your own spiritual and creative inclinations, whatever they may be, to bring light to your path of discovery. It should be noted that within the realm of using personal magic and creative expression with genealogy also comes the responsibility to maintain research standards that allow results to withstand scrutiny and to be useful for descendants in the future who seek us, their ancestors!

Whether your genealogy story is one told of genealogical and genetic connections, or one of a family created by choice, genealogy can be spiritual, magical, fun, and creative but it should also be nonfiction, even if the story isn't always pretty. The work of searching will likely be extremely tedious and frustrating too, and it does every genealogist well to remember that eventually our perseverance will yield a most precious gift: profound and meaningful ancestral connections and the precious knowledge needed to document genealogical truths in a manner of our choosing.

May you find those whom you seek, may your truths be heard, and may your genealogy journey be filled with magic along the way!

1

Preparing for Your Genealogy Journey

All journeys have secret destinations of which the traveler is unaware.

—Martin Buber

Choosing to embark on any journey requires preparation and planning, and the path of genealogy magic is no different. I've always been of the firm belief that my magic lies within—I don't do the magic, I am the magic—and I know I can do whatever magic I need to do with only myself. However, my path is a lot more enjoyable and fulfilling for me if I'm able to have certain tools with which to work and when I'm surrounded by a beautiful aesthetic. I'm a very visual person, and I love sitting within, or next to, a warm and inviting space that I've created with joy and intention. I love crafting oils and incense blends, dressing candles, decorating altars, playing in the garden, and working closely with nature and the moon, sun, and stars. We are blessed to exist in our human form on a planet infused with magic and energy beyond our comprehension and to use these goddess-given gifts as part of a magical practice is essential for me.

When I first began my genealogy journey, my initial approach was messy and slapdash. I had no plan. "Who needs a plan?" said this dramatic Leo sun with the impulsive Aries moon! There was no contingency for what I should do if things went sideways. Actually, I didn't even know things could go awry in genealogy, likely because I stepped into it from a very privileged position: white, cisgender, straight, unrestricted access to my birth record, and raised with genealogical family. For many years I wandered all around cyberspace, squandered time on frivolous research, scribbled bits of info in random notebooks and on other scraps of paper which often got lost, and half the time I forgot where I'd been online and what I wanted to do. I wasted time, replicated research, and overall, it just wasn't a good way to work. I also randomly included magic in my genealogy endeavors, but, again, there was no plan, no organization.

In 2013, I decided to begin the journey in earnest to discover my adopted husband's roots and his genealogical family of origin. He'd tested with 23andMe and, among his health results, came the surprise that he carries a genetic mutation for cystic fibrosis (CF), which is a disease of the lungs that is historically fatal by midlife and, if two carriers reproduce, can be passed down to genetic offspring. As a medical professional of many years, this startled me terribly, as my husband and I share children and grandchildren and CF is a hereditary disease. Although none of them had been diagnosed with CF, they could be carriers and, if they were, one day my grandchildren might have a child with someone who is also a carrier, and possibly pass down this terrible disease. In years prior, my husband and I had toyed around with trying to find his genealogical family of origin, and we occasionally engaged in half-hearted attempts, but he didn't really feel a strong pull to find out more. With the revelation of this genetic mutation, we both felt an urgent need to learn about his 50 percent of our children's genetics. I also realized that my approach had to be different this time—methodical, organized, and practical instead of sloppy and impulsive—and so I decided to apply the principles of my daily magical practice to genealogy.

It's said that to create a habit, one must do something daily for an average of sixty-six days. I'd reinvented my spiritual routine a few years before starting on my own genealogy magic journey, after sitting at the feet of a wise teacher who stressed the importance of a daily practice as an integral part of walking a magical path. The process of manifesting that comforting magical routine in my life served as my starting point for my determination to do genealogy the right way, and to include a core part of myself: my magic. I drafted a plan and set goals. I started using a journal to document my journey. I bought software to help me keep track of sources as I placed people on my tree. I incorporated a fixed set of magical tools and a routine for their use in my daily genealogy work. I gave myself permission to venture outside the boundaries of my routine only after I'd done the planned bits first, and I blessed my endeavor to journey into my family's genealogy with a ritual of beginning. My commitment to my genealogy started as a concerted effort and then morphed into a routine that is much more beneficial overall.

Magical Supplies for Starting Your Genealogy Magic Journey

While it is true that the only thing you really need for magic is yourself, it's always nice to have intentionally chosen supplies on hand. When I set out on my new-and-improved genealogy journey, I thought about the items I used frequently. I am an impulsive, grab whatever's at hand sort when it comes to doing magical work, so it was a bit challenging to think about, then write down, how I tossed little bits of magic into my genealogy. It took some time, but I was finally able to make a fairly complete list. From that, I created a toolbox of sorts from which I can select what I need, depending on the task at hand.

As you begin your journey, consider creating your own genealogy magic toolbox. It doesn't have to physically be an actual toolbox, of course, but perhaps you might like to keep these items in a drawer or, like me, a basket. Keeping them separate from your other magical supplies will help to keep them charged for the intent of using them for genealogy, and there's always the convenience of having them in one location.

Here is a starter list of suggested items. Feel free to incorporate your own preferred items as well.

Invest in a beautiful journal to the best of your financial ability and preference. If I had to make only one suggestion, this would be it. A notebook is fine too; that is what I use for much of my own work, especially the scribbly stuff I produce while actively researching that eventually gets transcribed into sensible writing. In addition to providing you with a place to document your feelings, insights, and intuitive ponderings along the way, a journal is also a place where you can record your research plans, keep a to-do list, and keep track of the websites you've visited, along with your discoveries. Some people choose to use multiple journals: one for reflection, and another for the documentation aspects. Choose what you think will work best for you but starting out with one journal is fine. I also suggest keeping a selection of pens, markers, and highlighters on hand. If you're a technology sort, a cyber-journal might work best for you, although I still do suggest keeping a paper-and-pen journal of some sort. Sometimes there's no replacement for the physical act of writing!

Create a sacred space in which to do your magic and ritual. This sacred space can be temporary, such as clearing off an end table in your living room and resetting it when you're done. (This is especially good for scenarios like roommates, or for homes that have frequent visitors, and when privacy is desired.) The sacred space can also be a permanent, dedicated space reserved just for your genealogy work, or it can take up a section of another altar on which you do other work.

Define the boundaries of your sacred space with an altar cloth. I've found this key ingredient necessary for me with any sacred space in which I work. It is simply a piece of cloth that is used on top of a surface to serve as a base on which other magical items will sit. I have a selection of square cloths that I use, however, my preferred is a vintage, ornately embroidered table runner that I found at a yard sale. Its beauty adds to the ambiance of my space, and I like how it gives me the feeling of another time.

Keep at least one candle on hand. Depending on the work to be done, I use a chime or spell candle, taper candle, seven-day candle, or a pillar candle. Tealights are also handy for quick work. If you must choose only one candle, get a seven-day candle, as this is what you will light each time you do genealogy. I feel it's the safest kind of candle as it's self-contained and usually works for any space. It's also a bit more cat-resistant but, depending on the cat, your mileage may vary!

Use crystals to manifest a magical vibe. As fragments of the earth, they speak to me of times gone by, of ancient history, and they offer a way to connect through their energy. Each crystal is its own resonator and, I'd even venture to say, has its own personality! It's likely that many readers will have at least one crystal already, and you might have one in mind. For those who want a suggestion, I propose a clear quartz palm stone as the first crystal in your genealogy magic toolbox. I use a crystal quartz palm stone as a centerpiece in the ancestral grids I construct (which will be covered later), and I like to hold it while meditating. I also hold it to infuse it with intent prior to magical work. Simply with its presence on an altar, it serves as a cleanser of energy and an amplifier of magic. Remember to cleanse your stone on a regular basis, with moonlight, sunlight, salt, or a quick rinse in running water (and then pat dry). I like to put mine on the window-sill when the moon is full. I set it there with the intention that it be cleared of any accumulated negativity and recharged with positive energy. For those who prefer not to work with crystals, look instead for flowers, rocks, and other natural items that resonate with you.

Finally on this starter list of magical tools are a clearing spray and an anointing oil. I find it helps me focus my intention when I cleanse the energy of my space with a clearing spray and use an anointing oil on my candle prior to lighting it. They set the mood for the space with both energy and intent. When it comes to genealogy magic, my first go-to is always rosemary (Salvia rosmarinus). It's my favorite because it is simultaneously clearing, protective, and its scent physically triggers the brain's memory center. Well-known as the "herb of remembrance," it, of course, smells fantastic. You can buy pre-made spray and oil from many places online and in person, but I've always enjoyed using the ones I've made with my own hands.

Recipes and Rituals

If you feel inclined to craft your own, here are two basic recipes for spray and oil. Feel free to change up the recipe in a way that feels best for your own magic, and please do so especially if you have a known sensitivity to rosemary or its essential oil. Some people choose to wear gloves when working with essential oils. I will leave that decision to you.

Prior to your blending, light a small candle and say:

Bless these hands and bless the work they are about to do. Infuse this spray/oil with the energies needed to manifest powerful magic and serve the highest good for all. May it be so.

Rosemary Clearing Spray
Ingredients and Materials:
   Glass bottle with spray cap, 4-ounce capacity
   Distilled water, 2 ounces
   Witch hazel, 2 ounces
   Rosemary essential oil, 27 drops
   Rosemary sprig, dried (optional)
   Isopropyl alcohol and a cloth or napkin
   Funnel

Instructions:
If you're going to use it, insert the dried rosemary sprig into the glass bottle. Add the rosemary essential oil. Using the funnel, add the distilled water and

witch hazel to the glass bottle. Cap the glass bottle and gently rotate. Wash your hands, then wipe down the outside of the bottle with isopropyl alcohol to disperse any oil on the outside. Be sure to give the bottle a gentle shake prior to each use.

As you spray your sacred space for clearing, do so with the intention that the space will be cleared of negativity and a welcoming, open space will be created.

Rosemary Anointing Oil

Ingredients and Materials:

> Carrier oil of your choice, one ounce (approximately 2 teaspoons)—
>> my favorite is sweet almond oil, but other good choices
>> include olive oil, coconut oil, grapeseed oil, and jojoba oil
> Rosemary essential oil, 9 drops
> One-ounce glass bottle with roller or dropper top
> Isopropyl alcohol and a cloth or napkin
> Plastic pipette
> Optional: a very small quantity of clear quartz chips—
>> I like multiples of 3, so perhaps 3, 6, or 9

Instructions:

If you're going to use clear quartz chips, add them to the glass bottle. Next, using the plastic pipette, add the carrier oil to the glass bottle until it's nearly to the top. Then, add the rosemary essential oil. Pop on the roller or dropper top and be sure it's firmly applied or you'll spring a leak. Cap the bottle and rotate it gently to disperse the essential oil in the carrier oil. Wash your hands, then wipe down the bottle with isopropyl alcohol to disperse any oil on the outside. Be sure to rotate the bottle gently prior to each use.

Again, store these items together, perhaps in a basket, to keep them energetically associated with each other and to maintain their purpose.

Open and Close Your Sessions

With each session of genealogy work, it is important to remember you are working with and within the spiritual realm. Plan to keep boundaries to firmly define when you are receptive to incoming information and energy. I do this by opening and closing my work times with a short prayer of blessing and thanks. To open, I light my orange seven-day candle and say these words:

Beloved Ancestors, I call to you now and ask for your love and wisdom as I walk this path of genealogy magic. Bless this work, that it opens the door to knowledge and serves the highest good for myself and others. May it be so.

Feel free to use my words or write your own as suited to your preference. Opening the work seems to be easy to remember, just don't forget to close when you are done! Often, I am back and forth between genealogy work and other daily activities, so I created the habit to snuff my work candle and close at the end of the day. I say these words:

My work is complete for today. Thank you for your guidance, and farewell for now.

Again, use my words, or write something that better suits you. Just be sure to open and close each session with intent.

A Ritual of Beginning

As a witchy woman who loves ceremony, a ritual of beginning came naturally to me when I decided to reorganize and work with genealogy purposefully and with a plan. I felt called to create a starting boundary, a point of initiation, a ceremonial dedication to walking the path of genealogy magic. Dedicating to something magically, for me, is an irrevocable act. It creates a firm statement to my conscious and subconscious selves, to Goddess, and to the universe, that I am committing myself to the responsibilities of acting in the highest good of all, and that I hold myself to that standard to the best of my ability. We all make commitments in life: as partners, parents, workers, activists, to the gods and goddesses to whom we felt a calling, to the world. Every promise is a commitment, it's a dedication to act authentically and with integrity.

With my ritual of beginning, I opened the door to a world of wonder, connections, and a feeling of wholeness that I'd never experienced. Even with the surprise of uncovering family secrets that would (temporarily) decimate my family tree as I'd always known it, I was able to move beyond the stories I'd been told and began to make real connections. I became a genealogical pilgrim on a spiritual quest to discover the names of the people who passed down the parts that make me whole, and to learn their stories. I created (and I'm still creating) a road map of the past for those yet to come so they too can make their own connections. I discovered the love of my ancestors across the generations. I now travel with purpose—I call myself a tree traveler—so I can sink my toes into the dirt of the ancestral homelands and feel the rush of belonging as it surges through me from root to crown. I stand strong in the knowing that I carry in my bones and my blood the innate right to exist on this earthly plane just as I am. I walk this path with joy and devotion and will continue to do so until I draw my last breath and join the ranks of the mighty dead.

If you feel called to walk the path of genealogy magic, consider starting the journey with your own ritual of beginning. The intention of this ritual is to open the door to a genealogy practice that is deeply meaningful, fulfilling, and healing. It is also a commitment that you dedicate yourself to walking the path with integrity, authenticity, an open mind, respect, compassion, and a pursuit of the truth. You may wish to review the section on ethics, guidelines, and standards prior to this ritual of beginning. As is the way on any magical path, you should always do what works best for you, so feel free to tweak the materials or wording to your own preference.

Materials:

*Taper or chime/spell candle in the color of your
     choosing—I like white for beginnings*
Seven-day candle, orange

Clearing spray (or incense, if that is your preference)
Anointing oil of your choice, skin-safe
Clear quartz palm stone, cleansed
Candle scribe
Candle snuffer
Mirror

Instructions:

Create a small altar dedicated to this ritual. If you're new to altar-building, start simple by choosing a flat space in an area where a candle can safely burn. Place a cloth on the surface to define the boundary of the sacred space and set your items on top of the cloth.

Mindfully clear the space by misting with a clearing spray. As you mist the space, set the intention that any energy that remains will be positive, joyful, and loving.

Once the space is cleared and intention set, stand at your altar or work-space. Use the candle scribe to carve your preferred name into the candle, starting at the base. Anoint the candle with the anointing oil; start at the base and move upward from base to top three times. By starting at the base and going in an upward motion, you are energetically sending your commitment out into the world. As you carve and anoint, state out loud:

My name is _____ (use preferred name). I stand here now, with respect and love, and ask those now gone and those yet to come to bear witness as I dedicate myself to the sacred path of genealogy magic.

Light the candle, stand (or sit) in front of the mirror and examine your unique and one-of-a-kind face for a few moments. While holding the palm stone in your dominant hand, close your eyes and manifest a large tree in your mind. See the leaves connected to the branches, the branches connected to the trunk. With your mind's eye, follow the trunk as it moves downward into the ground, to the roots that are spread wide and deep in the fertile earth. The roots reach outward in every direction, creating physical and energetic pathways to the roots of other trees. Briefly consider your genea-logical ancestors, those from whom you are descended by blood. If there is a feeling of emotional pain, do your best to push it aside and concentrate on the generations of ancestors beyond the ones who have caused you this hurt. Reflect on others in your life that you consider family, those with whom you have created a loving unit. Also think on the people, whether known to you personally or not, that have positively influenced you in such a way as to leave an impact on you that ripples outward with your words and actions. See the energy of all your people within this tree, feel the connections as they expand outward into the world, and allow the glittering web of inter-connectedness to settle upon your shoulders like a warm cloak. Read the following aloud, speaking the words with the intent to commit to a path of heartfelt purpose and righteous action for yourself and, if you choose to do so, for your work on behalf of others, both living and deceased.

These are the commitments that I will hold sacred and will do my best to uphold:

I commit to walking this path with integrity and authenticity.

I commit to a best effort to avoid harm with my words and deeds.

I commit to create and hold the boundaries I need to keep emotionally healthy as I do this work.

I commit to honor and maintain the privacy of others.

I commit to always be open to learning so that I walk this path with ever-increasing knowledge.

I commit that I will maintain an ethical standard that serves the highest good of all.

I commit that I will be compassionate and nonjudgmental.

I commit to the pursuit of facts and truth,
even when it's not the easiest path.

I speak these words aloud with the sincere hope that my walk on this sacred path will be blessed by those now gone and those yet to come, and by Goddess (or insert deity of choice, or none). May it be so.

Use the taper candle to light the orange seven-day candle and say these words aloud:

With the energy of the flame that has been lit as I begin my journey on this sacred path, I light this candle. May it serve as a source of inspiration and clarity, and as a reminder of my commitments to this work, every time it is lit.

Allow the taper candle to burn down. While the seven-day candle is lit, take some time to reflect and write your feelings about the beginning of this journey in your genealogy journal. When you are done, snuff the seven-day candle and close the sacred space to any lingering ancestral energy by saying,

This ritual of beginning is now complete. Thank you for your guidance, and farewell for now.

Blessings upon you as you undertake this sacred journey of genealogy magic!

2

Ethics, Guidelines, and Standards

*Ethics is knowing the difference between what you
have a right to do and what is right to do.*

—Potter Stewart

To travel the path of genealogy means you hold the hearts and souls of others within the container of your cupped hands, much as one might cradle a delicate treasure. Genealogy is a sacred undertaking, and, within the larger scope of mainstream genealogy, there lies much magic to be discovered and experienced. As people who walk the path of magical living, we are called to do our utmost to ensure that best practices are met and that we share our knowledge of them with those who journey alongside us, even for a short time.

Ethics and standards should be considered in some form or fashion by everyone in every area of life, as we each have a responsibility to the world at large to contribute in a way that is positive and meaningful. This is especially important with genealogy, since we are handling the most sensitive information about people and their families. Genealogical missteps can, and do, cause irreparable harm to people. In the world of genealogy, the term *genealogist* is not only reserved for the professionals, but also meant to apply to anyone who researches and documents family history, who takes a DNA test for genealogy, or who offers advice on that topic to others, even if it's "just for family!" As with all things in magic, in everyday life we are expected to be responsible for ourselves, so ultimately it falls to the individual person to understand fully the ethics and standards that are expected of them. If you're reading this book, this likely applies to you.

What are Genealogy Standards?

Genealogy standards are the best practices for genealogy. "They enable all genealogists . . . to come as close as possible to what happened in history."[1] Standards in genealogy, when followed, help to prevent the spread of misinformation and instead perpetuate truths, even the simplest truth of, "I don't know." It's hard to not be able to answer the questions we have about an ancestor. We must consider that some things are meant to never be discovered. While that can be difficult to sit with, we must find a way to be okay with it and not resort to shoddy research or an acceptance of information that isn't quite true just so we can fill a space in our tree. When we cannot locate what is needed to complete a family tree, or to break down a brick wall that obscures information, we must trust the ancestral energy contained within our energetic DNA and use it to remind ourselves of our wholeness. When we work with the magic of genealogy, we are also making a soul commitment to best practices, and to uphold the standards of a magical practice that serves the higher calling of connection to the ancestors, to ourselves, and to those who are yet to exist but who are waiting for their time to walk an earthbound path.

Leaders in the mainstream genealogy community have developed standards with the intent to provide a guideline to best practices. There is also a set of standards for genetic genealogy, including references to purchases, recommendations, sharing information, writing articles about genetic genealogy testing, and DNA testing for ancestry purposes. These guidelines all serve as a resource for a genealogy practice that is based on integrity and pursuit of truth.

---

[1] Board for Certification of Genealogists, *https://bcgcertification.org*

Genealogy Proof Standards (GPS)

Much like the GPS (Global Positioning System) in our car or on our phone that can help us to navigate the city streets, backroads, and highways to arrive at a certain destination (perhaps a cemetery!), genealogy also has guidelines that serve as a map to ensure we navigate to accurate conclusions by showing us the correct path. These guidelines are known as the Genealogy Proof Standards or GPS. The National Genealogical Society says of the GPS that they are "a process developed by the Board for Certification of Genealogists to give genealogists a standard method that helps them to apply an evaluative process in building a family tree." While working on research and documentation, these standards should always be taken into consideration. Why? There's a saying that goes, "Without proof there is no truth." In genealogy, it's easy to collect names and random facts that may or may not be correct, and then stick them into a tree. That's a surefire way to fill your genealogy story with errors. Instead, you should choose to work methodically, with a plan, and cultivate an appetite for sources that support your research. This kind of "genealogical hygiene" will result in a tree, written report, or other conveyance of your story that reflects genealogical truths. Also, following a set of standards will help you to have confidence in your research and documentation. From the Board of Certification of Genealogists:

> *Both professional genealogists and casual family researchers need genealogy standards in order to get their genealogy right. Without standards, inaccuracies and myths can be created and perpetuated. Many of these errors can be avoided by working to genealogy standards.*

The purpose of the Genealogical Proof Standard[2] is to show the minimum required from a genealogist for their work to be considered credible.

---

[2] Board for Certification of Genealogists, *Genealogical Standards, 50th Anniversary Edition* (Nashville & New York: Ancestry Imprint, Turner Publishing, 2014), 1–3, and Thomas W. Jones, *Mastering Genealogical Proof* (Arlington, Va.: National Genealogical Society, 2013).

There are five elements to the Genealogical Proof Standard:

1. Reasonably exhaustive research has been conducted.
2. Each statement of fact has a complete and accurate source citation.
3. The evidence is reliable and has been skillfully correlated and interpreted.
4. Any contradictory evidence has been resolved.
5. The conclusion has been soundly reasoned and coherently written.

Any proof statement is subject to re-evaluation when new evidence arises.

> *The GPS overarches all of the documentation, research, and writing standards . . . and is applied across the board in all genealogical research to measure the credibility of conclusions about ancestral identities, relationships, and life events.*[3]

More information about the Genealogical Proof Standard can be found on the Board for Certification of Genealogists website.

Standards for Obtaining, Using, and Sharing Genetic Genealogy Test Results

Along with the Genealogy Proof Standards that are typically applied to written research and documentation, there are also standards that focus on DNA testing and genetic genealogy, although both sets of standards do have overlap. The Standards for Obtaining, Using, and Sharing Genetic Genealogy Test Results were crafted by leaders in the field of genetic genealogy and were presented during the First Annual SLIG (Salt Lake Institute of Genealogy) Colloquium in Salt Lake City, Utah, in 2015. These twenty-one standards serve as a resource to all genetic genealogists and cover the following topics:

---

[3] Board for Certification of Genealogists, *Genealogy Standards,* second edition (Nashville, TN: Ancestry, 2019), 1–3.

- Company Offerings
- Testing with Consent
- Raw Data
- DNA Storage
- Terms of Service
- Privacy
- Access by Third Parties
- Sharing Results
- Scholarship
- Health Information
- Designating a Beneficiary
- Unexpected Results
- Different Types of Tests
- Y-DNA and mtDNA Tests
- Limitations of Y-DNA Testing
- Limitations of mtDNA Testing
- Limitations of Autosomal DNA Testing
- Limitations of Ethnicity Analysis
- Interpretation of DNA Test Results
- DNA as Part of Genealogical Proof
- Citing DNA Test Results[4]

Genealogist's Code of Ethics

Lastly, the Board for Certification of Genealogists has an excellent website that goes into a lot of detail about ethics and standards when working with genealogy. Among their resources is a code of ethics for genealogists. It is a

---

[4] You can download or read the detailed document online at *www.geneticgenealogystandards.com*

detailed document that reminds us of our obligation to always walk the path of integrity in all our endeavors. The Genealogist's Code of Ethics can be found on the Board for Certification of Genealogists website. Please read it and commit to a firm code of ethics for your own genealogy work.

A complete list of ethics, guidelines, and standards created by various genealogical societies and organizations can be found on the ISOGG wiki.[5] This comprehensive list contains the resources you need to enjoy genealogy while also manifesting a practice that is based on sound principles.

Again, please take the time to review these various ethics, guidelines, and standards. I know it's not a terribly exciting read, but this information is very important, for the simple fact that well-meaning people have caused great harm to others by sharing misinterpretations of genetic genealogy results or previously unknown information. Others lose their way by disrespecting privacy and acting in ways that do not reflect an ethic of integrity. Even if you are working only with your own DNA test results and family tree, these guidelines are in place to serve as a guide so you know the best way to handle any situation that arises, and adherence to them should be part of walking the path of genealogy magic.

---

[5] ISOGG wiki: *https://isogg.org*

3

The Language of Genealogy

*Language is the road map of a culture. It tells you where
its people come from and where they are going.*

—Rita Mae Brown

On my first consideration of writing about clear and concise communication within a genealogy framework, I thought it would be simple. We are who we are, after all, and that is what should be researched and documented. Unfortunately, that is not always the way of things, and within the history of genealogy and the language it uses to identify and address people, it leaves a lot to be desired. Genealogy doesn't always consider those who cannot access information. It makes assumptions, and its regimented nature can cause some to feel like genealogy has nothing to offer them. There doesn't seem to be much magic within this section of the book until you stop to think about the magic of words. Not much is more magical than the ability to share with one another the bits and pieces of ourselves, no matter the topic! It's essential to consider how our words and actions can influence others, especially within the realm of genealogy, and how the magic of this path can be affected by our choices as we walk it.

Historically, the language of genealogy has been heterocentric, primarily attuned to cis male/cis female couplings with genetic children and focused on the genealogical family. Regarding research, accessibility to records is limited or completely off-limits for many people due to circumstance, historical documentation practices, or both. Individuals are denied information due to family dysfunction, their family's refusal to accept certain aspects of their identity, lack of communication or knowledge, or all of the above. Others are denied access to information due to their status related to their mother's surrendering of them at birth, whether consensually or non-consensually. There are many other situations that result in people who don't have what they need to construct an accurate story of their own heritage. As a result, certain groups of people can be considerably disenfranchised and misrepresented within the framework of genealogy and its accompanying tools for discovering and recording information. While we cannot fully escape history, family dynamics, the documents of the past, or the facts of basic genetics, we can, and should, choose now to document and communicate in a way that shows an acceptance of all people, as well as demonstrate a sincere effort to be inclusive and to share what we know with those who have less information due to circumstances beyond their control.

Writing in a way that is inclusive can be a struggle, no matter the good intent. One of my goals in writing this book was to communicate in a manner that would demonstrate that genealogy is for everyone no matter the circumstances of birth, gender, sex, sexuality, religion, ability, or natural innate state of being. My mistake was in thinking it would be easy, however, words have limits that have been set in place by their use in society. Standards don't easily change, and using old words in a new way can limit how they're understood because people lose context. The need to quantify and define a group, for example, will invariably leave out some individuals who society would generally deem as belonging, or not, within the confines of the usual definition of said group. For instance, the word *man* generally means one thing in genealogy—an adult individual who was noted to have the appearance of male genitalia and therefore was assigned male at birth—but, to a trans person, that standard genealogical definition of man can leave them feeling set apart.

It takes anywhere from ten to twenty years for a word to come into common use, and altering how words are perceived also takes time.

Thankfully, this process of expanding ideas and broadening and redefining words has already begun within the wider realm of genealogy. Genealogists understand deeply the immense power of family, of connections, and many are now working on ways to help genealogy be more expansive and inclusive for those who don't fall within the spectrum of cis- and hetero-centric lived experiences. It's very complicated and will likely take quite some time to manifest. Meanwhile, there remains a heavy reliance on current standards and definitions with the hope that people who fall outside their narrow scopes can somehow still find a way to fit themselves in, at least until new standards are outlined and defined for use within the larger genealogical community. It's imperfect at best, but, again, change is on the horizon.

The Language of Genealogy for Adoptees and Others Searching

For those who don't have contact with or information about their genealogical family of origin, genealogy can seem pointless, especially when the work is focused on the genealogical family. For many years, there's been a movement to open records for adopted people to learn the name of their genetic parents. It's been a difficult struggle. As of this writing, only in a limited number of states in the United States can adult adoptees, openly and without restriction, access their own original birth records. In many closed states, adult adoptees are often forced to petition the court system for access to their own records, and even worse, they often need a valid reason to have them opened, such as a sick child, or a terminal illness. Why should anyone need to be dying, or have a sick child, to see their original birth records? Most people don't think about their certificate of birth. They can access it without issue. For adult adoptees, the challenge can often be insurmountable. This is unacceptable and needs to change. Adoptee advocacy organizations like Bastard Nation work tirelessly to bring about the legal changes needed so that every adult has equal access to their own birth information without needing to jump through hoops to legitimize their need for it.

There are generations of adults who were placed for adoption at birth and who still cannot access the details surrounding their birth. Birth records were originally altered and sealed to protect the surrendered child from being identified and found by the birth mother, or to shield the adoptive family from the shame of not being able to have a genetic child, or both. It was not done to provide privacy or to shield the identity of the birth mother. It is a misconception at best to assume that birth mothers want to be protected from their own children. Lorraine Dusky writes on her [Birth Mother] First Mother Forum blog, "Taken together, surveys from various countries where access to original birth certificates is granted, including those states in the United States, show that 95 percent of birth mothers welcome contact and wanted reunion."

In my own research and advocacy work, I've found that there seems to be a common thread of shame and secrecy among birth mothers who gave birth in the 50s, 60s, and 70s. Often, these young women were sent away by their family to have their babies in secret, they were threatened, they were lied to, they were forced to give away their babies against their wishes. Why? Largely due to patriarchal moral standards that penalized women for engaging in consensual sexual intercourse outside the confines of marriage. For those who did not consent, it was even more harsh, as far too often victims of sexual assault are assumed to have somehow "asked for it" by dint of their clothing or behavior choices. It was, and remains, a harmful and inaccurate rhetoric. Especially among white families in the United States, no matter the circumstances of conception, an unwed pregnant daughter was considered a blemish on the family's good reputation. This ridiculous notion was perpetuated by society in general as they spoke poorly of, and ostracized, families who did not keep their daughters in line.

Within genealogy, the process of how information is shared with documentation such as birth certificates, and in family trees, for example, is such that whatever is accessible within the written record is considered and accepted as fact. For adoptees, the accessible records are too often falsehoods. Sadly, and infuriatingly, the prevailing attitude among many people is that adult adoptees are expected to just be thankful that they weren't aborted, and that a good family stepped up to take care of them. All too often it's implied they're not supposed to want to find their genealogical family of origin because to do so implies a lack of satisfaction with their (adoptee) life. They're supposed to be grateful, and that's it. When queries are made by adult adoptees to DNA matches, mentioning adoption can be the trigger that causes people to not respond, to delete information from their profiles and, in some instances, to delete their test results so that the adult adoptee does not discover information.

Before she hung up on me, I was told by the elderly sister of my mother's genetic father, "I have enough family." My mother wasn't seeking money, or even to be given a label as a member of the family, she just wanted to see a picture of her paternal grandmother, a long-deceased woman to whose face my mother and I are said to bear an uncanny resemblance. A man told me via email when I was working to find my adopted husband's genealogical family, "I don't want to be the one who lets this skeleton out of the closet." These scenarios were very different: my mother was searching for a genetic parent she didn't know existed until she was sixty-four years old, and my adopted-at-birth husband was searching for genealogical family to obtain a medical history, but the received responses left a similar feeling of rejection. I don't think people intentionally mean to be unfeeling, however, words spoken or written in response to an adoptee's contact can be knee-jerk, cold, and uncaring, and they can feel hostile. Sadly, the responses I received were based on the outdated patriarchal morality of women needing to remain "pure and untouched" by a man until they were firmly within the confines of marriage, and the misinformation that has been perpetuated that birth mothers need to be saved from being contacted by their children.

The language of genealogy for adult adoptees and others searching should be based in compassion. Those walking the path of genealogy magic, especially when using DNA testing as an adjunct to research, need to do so with the knowledge that they might uncover previously unknown knowledge.

Attached to the other end of a "secret" is usually a person with feelings, with hopes and dreams, who is searching to find out more. Sometimes the person we discover is one for whom we've been searching, except they don't know they're being sought. This happens with fathers who don't know they've fathered children. Other times the person is searching for any information, and we hold the information, or we have knowledge of shared genetic connections, that will bring resolution to their quest to find out more. Either way, compassion is key. Mind your words and consider that another person's existence and their innate right to know the truth of their heritage, genealogy, and genetics should take precedence over outdated morality and the horrid concepts of secrecy and shame. When in doubt, always refer to and rely on the standards set by the genealogical community to guide you on best practices.

The Language of Genealogy for the LGBTQIA+ Community

*The power of language to shape our perceptions of other people
is immense. Precise use of terms in regards to gender and sexual
orientation can have a significant impact on demystifying many
of the misperceptions associated with these concepts.*

—PFLAG

In addition to adoptees and others searching, the LGBTQIA+ community also feels negative effects from the currently accepted standard terms and vocabulary that we use in genealogy. There is an active movement within the genealogy community, especially among Gen Z genealogists, to create and commit to using a standardized set of terminology that is more inclusive to LGBTQIA+ people, accepting each individual as they identify, while also aligning as necessary with the scientific aspects of genetic genealogy. I must be clear, though: it is a challenge. Every person, without exception, should be able to identify and openly live as their mind, body, and soul compels them. The fact also remains that we each come into the world with a distinct genetic makeup that, barring genetic variations,[6] places each of us within an XX or XY designation, with X and Y each having its own specialized functions that cannot be ascribed to the other. Put simply, how we identify does not change our genetic composition. Finding a balance that supports each person's identity while keeping to the science of genetic genealogy will take time, but I am optimistic that it is forthcoming.

Within all its bells and whistles, genealogy also serves as a written record of human reproduction. Two people connect, whether through sexual intercourse or, in our modern times, some other way of impregnation, sperm fertilizes egg, a person carries and births one or more infants, and the facts of this are documented with names, sexes, dates, and times. It seems straightforward. However, what is documented doesn't always match who some people are within their being. Since we don't get to choose what sex we're assigned at birth, we're designated as either female or male based on the appearance of our external genitalia. In writing about people during research and documentation, the acronyms *AFAB* and *AMAB* are terms to consider. They mean, respectively, "assigned female at birth" and "assigned male at birth" and are preferred over terms like "biological female/male" and "born female/male." Occasionally babies are born with ambiguous genitalia that doesn't clearly define their sex. Testing is done before sex is assigned or, sometimes, the parents must choose.

As an infant grows into a toddler and beyond, hints of their gender begin to emerge. *Gender* is defined as a set of social, psychological, and emotional traits that classify a person as a man, a woman, a mixture of both, or neither. It is important to remember that gender is not the same as sex (although there is overlap) and, just as we have no choice over the sex we're assigned at birth, neither is our gender a choice. It simply is what it is. A person's sense of

---

[6] The topics of genetic variations on XX and XY, such as XXX, XXY, and XYY, and other scenarios, such as three parent individuals, or XY females and XX males, fall outside the scope of this book. However, please do research to find out more!

being a girl or woman, a boy or man, some of both, and neither, is known as *gender identity*. As we grow, we fall into our gender identity naturally, usually around age four, but children as young as eighteen months old have shown awareness of their own gender identity. For some people, their gender does not always match their assigned sex. In a better world, a person would be able to state their gender and accompanying pronouns and that would be the end of it. However, that's not the case, and most of us know of someone who has had to fight to be accepted on their own terms. When we write within the framework of genealogy, the term *affirmed gender*, which is the gender by which a person wishes to be known, should replace terms like chosen gender, which implies that a person's gender was chosen rather than it simply being in existence.

The standard, and narrow, definition of family that seems to still pervade much of society's hive mind doesn't begin to accommodate all the ways families are built and exist. Some years ago, I'd have described myself as a woman married to a man and together, we have two daughters. The language has changed. While I personally don't have an issue with my previous description, using it in some contexts can imply that it's the norm. When I say instead, "I am a hetero-cis female who identifies as a woman, I am married to a hetero-cis male who identifies as a man, we share two children who were assigned female at birth and who each currently identify as hetero-cis female," then I am identified in a way that insinuates that other options are open and exist. For those who are disenfranchised or excluded because they identify in a non-hetero, non-cis manner, this change in wording, or at least an open-minded approach to hearing and reading it, can be meaningful and offer an atmosphere of acceptance.

Another topic that comes up is that of the *dead name*. This is a name given at birth that is no longer used, by choice, most frequently by the LGBTQIA+ community but in other groups as well. Simply put, the person's name given to them at birth is dead to them. In speaking with members of the LGBTQIA+ community about the topic of dead names, it was apparent that there is a lot of pain for those with family and acquaintances who insist on using a dead name. I was told, "Being called by the name given to me at birth reminds of me of all the time I spent being someone else, when I couldn't be me." This person did not want their dead name used, ever, in any scenario. In genealogy, this could be considered to present a problem for accurate documentation. However, I believe with adequate additional documentation, like including the names of the person's parents, the lineage will be easily apparent for future researchers. For others who have a dead name, it's not quite so important that the name never come up. Another person shared, "My dead name doesn't represent me anymore, but it is part of my journey, and I won't repudiate it." Again, while this can complicate documentation on the surface, ultimately, we must conclude that people should be represented in the manner of their choosing, even when it means that future research might be made more challenging because of it. One train of thought in this scenario is to broadly document using the person's preferred name and affirmed gender, if that is a consideration, and make sure it's attached in various ways to the documentation of the family. The connections will be made, and the person's wishes are ultimately accepted.

The language of genealogy for the LGBTQIA+ community should be based in respect. It is our nature to make assumptions; however, in genealogy, that needs to change. If you're not sure about something, asking for clarification is sure to be appreciated. Choose to document in ways that are respectful of each person's innate being, even when it doesn't fall within what society would currently consider the norm. Be supportive of how chosen family is represented within a tree. Use their names as they request you to do so and apply the affirmed gender as they have shared it. If in doubt, don't enter a gender at all. There are many people within my tree whose gender identity is unknown. It does nothing to the authenticity of the tree to leave that box unchecked. Above all, respect privacy and choice.

The Language of Genealogy for Descendants of Enslaved Persons

Throughout recent history, we find written stories of enslaved people and those who enslaved them. Africa is one, but not the only, place from which enslaved persons were forced into bondage. However, in the context of this book and unless otherwise noted, "enslaved persons" generally refers to those who descend from people of African origin who were brought to the Americas against their will.

In discussing the history of slavery, it is especially important to consider how you use the words that commonly surround the subject. In the Owens-Thomas House & Slave Quarters in Savannah, Georgia, there is a text panel that summarizes quite succinctly how and why our word choices matter so much:

> *Words have Power. They express meanings, ideas, and relationships. They impact how we relate to the past and one another. As we share this history, we strive to use words that are empathetic to those whose history has been marginalized. For example, we use phrases like enslaved woman, rather than slave. The noun slave implies that she was, at her core, a slave. The adjective enslaved reveals that though in bondage, bondage was not her core existence. Furthermore, she was enslaved by the actions of another. Therefore, we use terms like enslaver, rather than master, to indicate one's effort to exert power over another. You may hear other phrases like slave labor camp or escapee, rather than plantation or runaway. These reinforce the idea of people's humanity rather than the conditions forced upon them.*

In researching, you will find the documentation practices of the time usually relegated enslaved persons to the realm of household possessions, akin to furniture and livestock, often with a dollar value attached. Before 1870, censuses most often did not list enslaved persons by name, but rather listed them by assigned sex and age. In some probate records, there are first names of enslaved persons recorded, however, this information all too often doesn't help when researching a family line. After emancipation, formerly enslaved persons sometimes kept the surname of their enslavers, but some also changed their surname to one of preference to create an identity of their choosing. Again, this can make research quite challenging, and many African Americans are unable to trace some, or all, of their lines beyond the census of 1870.

In the United States, most people associate slavery only with the South, but it was a part of colonial life in the North as well. Northern merchants made hefty profits from the transatlantic triangle trade of molasses, rum, and slaves. At one point, more than forty thousand enslaved persons toiled in cities and on farms across northern Colonial America. One-fifth of New York City's population was enslaved in 1740. While abolitionists, anti-slavery activists, and opponents in the North worked to abolish the slave trade much earlier than in the South, it does everyone well to remember that having ancestry only in the northern United States does not give an automatic pass to having enslaver ancestors in the family tree.

In my own family history, I have one known line of ancestors that enslaved people. I know this because of documents such as a transcription of a case that went before the Arkansas Supreme Court, census "slave schedules," and other sources of information. In addition, I have DNA matches to people of color whose online profiles indicate they are researching enslaved ancestors, some of whom carry the surnames of my enslaver ancestors. It's an ugly legacy and one that I didn't want to think too deeply about for a long time. It was only when I was contacted by a genetic cousin for information about a possible shared ancestor that I began to realize the importance of communication, and of sharing information. Let me state this firmly: Feeling horror, embarrassment, and sadness at descending from ancestors who enslaved others does not supersede the ethical obligation to share what is known with descendants of enslaved persons who are searching. We must evolve, learn, and do better. The work of researching on behalf of, and in conjunction with, DNA cousins who are descendants of enslaved persons is now a very important part of my genealogy path, and I feel honored to work with them to uncover answers. The magic of genealogy really shines when the damaged roots of two trees connect and the shared lineage can begin the process of being adjusted and healed.

The language of genealogy when working within the context of history and enslaved persons should always take into consideration how we use our words, and an acknowledgment of harm done. If you have enslaver ancestors, go ahead and take a short bit of time to feel your feelings about it, then move on to doing something productive with the information. How can your knowledge of your family tree help someone else? Hiding, or attempting to hide, this ancestry does nothing to adjust the energy of past actions taken by ancestors. While I cannot erase the horrors inflicted by enslaver ancestors, I offer what I know to those who are seeking information and assist their effort wherever possible. I also choose to be open to hearing about other ways I can help. Enslaver ancestry is an ugly legacy. Those of us who descend from enslavers have an obligation to accept slavery's truths, acknowledge its continued harm to the descendants of enslaved persons, and its benefits to ourselves. We must do the work to heal and adjust our lineage in such a way that our descendants have an innate understanding of slavery's horrors and, with such knowing, will do what is needed to create and maintain an equitable world for all.

Social Considerations

Beyond the science of genetic genealogy, we also need to consider our definition of family and how social attitudes and constructs have influenced that. I think many of us have heard about, or participated in, the "family tree project" at the elementary school level, where students are encouraged to create a tree that shows their family. For some, this is an easy task and shows genetic siblings, Mom, Dad, Grandma and Grandpa, Mimi and Pops, and it's very straightforward. For others, it's not so simple. Families are often blended. There could be Mom, Dad, and a stepmom, half- and step-siblings.

There could be two gay dads, two lesbian moms, a trans dad, perhaps a child lives with Grandma or Aunt Sue, or they're in foster care and live with people who are no relation at all and therefore cannot, or don't want to, share their information. Some adopted people, like my husband, have shared that they sometimes felt a sort of isolation from the adoptive family—like they weren't "real family" within their family who are all genetically related—and projects like the family tree left them feeling disconcerted, disconnected, and alone in the world, adrift with no people of their own.

This leads us forward to the situations that adults face when researching and documenting their own genealogy. First, we cannot assume that what's written on a piece of paper is indeed a true fact. Documents can be altered, or misinformation entered, for any number of reasons. For example, birth certificates are considered a primary source of documentation in genealogy research. My husband has a birth certificate that shows the name of his adoptive parents in a way that, for those who aren't aware that he is adopted, states their names as a fact that they are his genetic parents. This is because when an infant or child is adopted, their original birth certificate is locked away and only the amended birth certificate, listing the adoptive parents' names, is available. Prior to the passage of Louisiana HB 450 (which provides for access to an adopted person's original birth certificate) in June 2022, my husband was denied access to the original birth certificate that documented his birth and the name of his genetic parents because Louisiana was not an open access state that allowed this document to be obtained. While researching his adoption, we reached out to the State of Louisiana for a non-ID which is a document that outlines medical and other information about the adoptee's birth mother, and sometimes the birth father, but does not give identifying information about them. In my husband's case, the non-ID gave a birth date different than the one on his amended birth certificate, and also said he was assigned female at birth. This is an example of how, for many years across the United States, there was an active campaign of sorts to ensure a complete separation of mother from infant by the manipulation of what is considered fact by means of official paperwork.

This fits what was done to millions of adoptees during what is known as the "Baby Scoop Era" that occurred from 1945 to 1973, and during which an estimated four million babies were surrendered for adoption. Documentation during this era, and even continuing into today, does not always reflect the true facts of an individual's birth. Perhaps you've seen a post on social media from an adoptee listing their birth date and location and asking for information about family? If you have unrestricted access to your birth information, take a moment to consider what it must be like to beg strangers for this basic information about yourself. The stories of loss, inability to access information, and scenarios of disconnection abound in many people, not just adoptees, and care must be taken to always be compassionate when walking the path of genealogy magic. The adage of walking a mile in someone's shoes definitely applies.

In addition to scenarios previously mentioned, there are some other vintage documents that can be quite valuable in genealogy research but that also can contain information that is incomplete, or just nonexistent, usually regarding women's surnames:

- Baptismal records often list the infant's mother by her married name, or only used her first name, or don't list her at all.

- Obituaries often listed surviving female relatives by their married name. For example, it is common to see "Mrs. John Jones" instead of Mary Smith Jones in old obituaries. In cases where the husband was deceased, sometimes "Mrs. Mary Jones" would be used, but still with no reference to her family name.

- Marriage documents will often list the bride's first name and the name of her father. The mother is either not mentioned or is mentioned by first name only, or with the surname of her husband.

There are a variety of scenarios in which individuals find themselves removed from the family circle. Marriage to someone outside the family's social class, religion, culture, or a mix of them, have been the impetus to treat a family member as if they were dead or nonexistent. Interracial marriage is another. Some people who fall within the cluster of the LGBTQIA+ letters were purposely pushed away from their genealogical family at a young age. One person with whom I spoke shared a story of resilience in the face of heartbreaking rejection. They were expelled from their family at the age of eighteen, their mother took their pictures out of the family album, their father offered them money to change their name and move out of state and, many years later, they were not listed as a survivor in their parents' obituaries. In short, their parents made every attempt to obliterate their existence from the family story. Regarding my question about what DNA testing might mean for the LGBTQIA+ community they told me, "For some queer people, DNA testing is the only way they'll ever find out anything about their genetic heritage." The person who shared this with me is married for many years now and has a loving family of choice, one created by bond instead of blood. Their family story is just as valid and important to the documentation of the human experience as a hetero-cis person's family story.

All these situations speak to the importance of DNA testing for those who want to explore their roots but don't have access to their family and its stories. It also reinforces that we must consider each person's story and their desire to record the facts of their life as it exists. In considering their family, and that of others with similar circumstances, we are reminded that there are many ways to have a family, all are valid, and each one represents a place on the beautiful spectrum of how families exist. Each one is worthy of writing down for the future to look back upon, much as we do now.

There are other factors to consider, and, while I don't have all the answers for how to handle them, I encourage each genealogist to think carefully about what will work best and serve the highest good for all involved. It is most important to remember that we should always respect the wishes of those we document and write about. Here is an example, and a question to consider:

Some people are legally changing their sex assigned at birth on their birth certificate and other legal documents after they transition. The change, contributes to the affirmation of gender, among other things, however, it doesn't change genetic facts. An XY trans woman will still carry within her genetics the Y-DNA that represents her father's paternal line, for example. The question then arises: What is the best way to represent a transgendered individual in a family tree? The short answer is that you represent them in the way they choose. If you don't know, ask! In these instances, especially, genetics must take second place, and the person, and their right to exist within their family tree and the world as their innate self, must take precedence.

The takeaway from all of this is that we should each make a concerted and heartfelt effort to write in a way that includes each person in the manner of their choosing, and how they identify. Genetic facts are important and cannot be changed, but, along with the science of the family story, there are the aspects of the day-to-day life to consider. It does well to remember that to fully tell a story, the people within it must be represented as their true and actual selves or there really is no truth to the story at all, is there?

Clear Communication
The best way to manifest an energy of clear and concise communication is to magically commit to it. Infusing a lapis lazuli with this intention, then keeping it near you as you work, helps to maintain this commitment.

Materials:
  Lapis lazuli
  Yellow chime/spell candle
  Clearing spray

Instructions:
Create a sacred space with a clearing spray and the intention that the space is filled with love and positive energy. Light the candle and hold the lapis lazuli in both hands, and say,

I endeavor to always communicate clearly and effectively from a place of honesty and compassion. May my words always carry love and truth with them.

Set the lapis lazuli in front of the candle and let the candle burn down. Keep the crystal next to your workspace, perhaps near your clear quartz crystal.

4

Family Story

If you cannot get rid of the family skeleton, you may as well make it dance.

—George Bernard Shaw

hat's your family story? This is the first question I ask every client. Before creating a plan to engage in DNA testing and research, I always assess the knowledge of the individual regarding their family history as they know it. The story of a family's origin is usually passed down through generations but much like the old game of Telephone there are nuances lost in the translation, assumptions are made, and it's often the case that the reality of a family's roots doesn't always match the story.

I am a prime example of someone who has lived with a family story that was woefully incorrect. I was raised in New Orleans with unfettered access to my mother's family and its stories of our roots, but did not have a regular connection with my father or his side of my family. As a result, I grew up with little knowledge of my father's family, but with a strong sense of cultural belonging in the Southeast Louisiana region in which many of my maternal ancestral lines have lived since their arrival in 1721. Family stories passed down by my maternal grandmother, the "old aunts" (her sisters), older cousins, and other extended family, led me to believe I was mostly French and Acadian, with a smattering of Scots Irish and English, and directly descended from President Zachary Taylor. What little I did know about my father's side of my family came from my grandmother. She said he had some German ancestry and may have been a descendant of the Blackfoot Confederacy. I had long, straight, dark hair, brown skin when I tanned, and dark eyes, so everyone thought that was right. I didn't identify culturally as Native American, but neither did I question any of this ancestral story for many years. I still have no idea of its origin. From where exactly did my grandmother hear that my father was a descendant of the Blackfoot Confederacy? She is gone now, and I've asked my mother, but she doesn't remember.

After the advent of direct-to-consumer DNA testing, I did my own testing and began a deep re-exploration into all the branches of my tree. I suspected there were some inaccuracies in my family's stories about our deeper origins. I also DNA-tested various family members. Eventually I uncovered family secrets that blew part of my family story into a million pieces and caused a lot of heartache. I'll share more about that later.

This photo of me as a small girl (with my baby sister Kelly and our dog Angel), and others like it that show me with dark skin, were often held up as "proof" that I descended from a Native American ancestor on my father's side.

Some people, whether because of adoption or another circumstance that has removed them from the knowledge of their own genealogical family tree, may have no story at all. My husband grew up with zero knowledge of his genealogical family of origin because he was placed for adoption at birth. The first time he met a person who was genetically related to him was at the birth of our oldest daughter. His family story, and his sense of identity, came from the family into which he was adopted. His adoptive father's side is French, his adoptive mother's side is mostly English, Irish, and Scottish, a blend that seems to occur frequently in those with Appalachian roots. Through DNA testing, we eventually discovered his recent genetic roots lay in the northern part of the United States, in Chicago, but he feels no pull to that part of the country or its culture. His cultural sense of self was forged in and around New Orleans and he is very much a part of its fabric, despite having no close genealogical connections in southeastern Louisiana. He and other adoptees, along with those who grew up away from their family of birth, are examples of the very powerful magic that lies within the family of influence.

Expulsion from the genealogical family is one of many scenarios that occur that keep people from the verbal retelling of family history, and it prevents them from asking questions, looking at pictures, participating in family traditions, and occasionally, feeling a part of the culture. One of the beauties of DNA testing is the reconnection it provides to our heritage. This is vitally important to the people who, for whatever reason, have been removed from the source that would give them information about their heritage, their roots, their own family story.

Regarding inaccurate family stories, the most common one I come across in the United States, and the one that is most strongly defended, is the assertion that an ancestor—a great-grandparent, or a great-great-grandparent—was "full-blooded Native American," usually Cherokee. As I mentioned, my own story also had a Native American ancestor on my father's side and I'm nearly 100 percent sure that is incorrect, at least on his side of my genetics. I did have one experience that has kept me from fully committing to my lack of Native American ancestry. Back in the early 2000s, I worked as a travel nurse. One assignment took me to the Southwest, where I stayed for many weeks. I worked in the ICU, and there was a Navajo elder and healer on staff who rounded daily on each patient that was a member of the local tribe. Hers was important work that made a big difference in how families coped with critical illness, and how patients recovered from it. On a day when I was caring for one of her patients, she approached me to discuss the patient, and the conversation ultimately turned to the spiritual, as it often does between magical people. During our talk, she mentioned to me that I have "Native blood." At the time, my hair was very long, and near to black and when I worked, I kept it pulled back in a long braid. I shared with her that my appearance sometimes led people to think that I was Native American, but that I really wasn't. She laughed and said, "But you are Native." I asked her how she knew that, and she replied, "I know you have Native blood in you because I see your ancestors standing behind you, and they are telling me so."

Her talk with me, which I keep within my heart and mind as valuable words of wisdom from a Navajo elder and wise woman, does still give me pause for reflection. The other, private, things she told me have indeed come to pass. I also have lines on my mother's side that are "brick walls," meaning I can't get past a certain ancestor. They're relatively recent—great-great-grand-parents—and they are from the area of Louisiana in which there is often found among the people a mix of French, Native American, and African heritage. I do have a tiny, and consistent, portion of my ethnicity result that is from Africa, and I also have French in my ethnicity result, so perhaps I descend from an ancestor who carried that particular mix of DNA and I just haven't inherited the Native American part of it? However, that's a stretch with no evidence, and I don't know that I will ever know for sure. I do know that I am not culturally Native American, and I consciously mind my words and actions so that I don't appropriate spiritual practices, dress, or anything else that is considered Native American. However, because of her words, I keep a small bit of earth on my altar to represent, and pay respects to, Native American ancestors that just might be within my energetic DNA (more on that later).

I've had clients totally dismiss their DNA tests as wrong or fake because the ethnicity portion didn't show any percentage of DNA from the Indigenous Americas. There are two reasons why an ethnicity estimate might not show any percentage from the Indigenous Americas: there isn't enough inherited DNA from a Native American ancestor to show in the ethnicity results, or there isn't really a Native American ancestor. In my experience, it is likely the latter but, as in my own case, sometimes we just don't know. It is important to remember that a lack of a particular ethnicity in our results doesn't necessarily mean we don't descend from certain people. We also need to keep in mind that having a positive ethnicity result doesn't entitle us to claim that culture and its particulars as our own. Ethnicity estimates are just that: estimates. The science is getting better, but it's still new. Ethnicity results are deemed accurate only at a continental level. They do not ever give us permission to appropriate a culture that isn't the one in which we were raised or trained. I also have Welsh DNA, a fair bit of it, but I am not Welsh. I am American with Welsh ancestry. I have a small and consistent percentage of African ethnicity but this does not mean I can appropriate spiritual or other practices that are associated with African culture. We should always be mindful of these distinctions.

For Americans, the lack of connection to the land on which many of us live as descendants of settlers and colonizers causes real emotional pain and contributes to the insistence by many people that they're genetically connected to the Indigenous Americas. I have a theory about why this happens: descendants of settlers and colonizers have no sense of spiritual connection with this land. Our deepest ancestry stories unfolded in lands that are thousands of miles away. When our ancestors emigrated from their homelands to the United States, we lost that connection to the lands of our own people because they left behind their lands, their dead, their culture. Much was brought with them, but it got lost or was blended into customs and cultures from other lands. As a result, we lost connection to the culture, we lost the overall sense of belonging to the larger stream of consciousness that flows forth from the land into its people. For some, this feeling of loss leads them to seek out a genetic connection to America's indigenous peoples and when that doesn't manifest, they are forced to really tune in to the loss.

There are ways to manage this that don't encroach on appropriation. Connecting via DNA testing to the genetic heritage we each have is a first step. Learning more about genetic family and our roots through traditional genealogy is another because it ultimately leads us to seek out the places from which our own people traveled. When I first discovered that I have a deep well of ancestral ties to Italy, my intense curiosity about Italian witchcraft made more sense to me. I am what is commonly referred to as an American mutt which is a bit of slang to indicate that I have ancestry from many places. My research does reflect this to be so, and so far I can trace ancestors to England, Scotland, Ireland, Wales, Cornwall, France, Germany, Poland, and Italy. I too have felt feelings of disconnection from the land on which I was raised, and this feeling is not uncommon as it has also been shared with me by many others who are also descended from ancestors who traveled.

One way that I manage these feelings is through travel of my own, and I am privileged to be able to do so. I call myself a "tree traveler" as most of my journeys are planned in places to which I have traced an ancestral line. The feeling of standing upon the ground on which an ancestor walked in years gone by is amazing, and it brings that feeling of connection to the fore. I enjoy wandering cemeteries and graveyards in those places and paying my respects to the people of that place. I support the culture of the place by spending my money on local lodging, food, and crafts made by local hands. I try to respectfully nab a tiny bit of the earth in the form of dirt, a small pebble, or a fallen leaf, so that I can place it upon my altar when I return home. This allows me to keep my feeling of connection and reminds me that I always carry that place within me. The blood and the bones remember.

Journal Magic: Your Family Story

I find it empowering and enlightening to write about family, both what I know and what I do not know. For this magical exercise, I want you to document what you know and what you don't know in this moment about your own family. Pull out your journal and pen. Light your candle, hold your writing crystal in your dominant hand, and remember to open your writing session with this short prayer, or one of your own choosing.

Beloved Ancestors, I call to you now and ask for your love and wisdom as I walk this path of genealogy magic. Bless this work, that it will open me to the stream of consciousness of ancestral knowledge and serve the highest good for myself and others. May it be so.

Place the writing crystal near the space where you're writing or place it in a pocket or purse if that's more convenient. Begin writing down the stories you've been told about your family. Start with your mother line. Where was your mother born? Her parents? Her grandparents? Her great-grandparents? Are there marriage stories? War stories? Interesting occupations? Is there a particular heritage to which they belong (Irish, German, Igbo, Chinese, Jewish, Italian, Syrian, for example)? Ask the same questions for your father line. Slowly work your way through your memories. If you're unsure, or suspect something might not be accurate, write it down anyway so you can explore your recollections in the future. Depending on your knowledge, this exercise might take a good bit of time.

Also write down what you don't know. For example, you might say, "I don't know anything about my dad's great-grandfather. That's always been a bit of a mystery and I'd like to know more." For some of you, writing down recollections of a family story might not take much time because you have little to no information. If that's the case, take this time to write a story about yourself, about where you think your deep ancestral roots might lie. Ponder any connections you feel to a certain part of your genealogical ancestry, or to any lands or spiritual traditions to which you've felt called but don't know why. As I mentioned, for many years I felt a call to explore Italian witchcraft, even though I had no known Italian ancestors. I later discovered through DNA testing some family secrets that ultimately led me to an Italian great-grandmother from southern Italy.

The beauty of genealogy and DNA testing is that it allows us to reconnect to our roots by providing us with clues. For all of us, and especially for those who are adopted, or who are disconnected from their genealogical family of origin for another reason, receiving DNA test results can be a magical experience. If you've tested your DNA and have ethnicity results to which you can refer, think on how the results matched, or didn't match, your family story. What feels familiar? Was anything a surprise? If so, what . . . and why? Write about your feelings and experiences in your journal. If they're negative, that's okay too. Later in the book we will discuss the magic that surrounds letting go.

The wonder of the family story is how its words connect us to the past, and to the people from whom we descend, with all their ways of being and the lessons they've passed along that have filtered down to us in snippets of wisdom that we likely don't recognize as being from anywhere in particular. For those without a family story, or who lack one for part of their tree, this loss of heritage can be painful or leave one feeling a bit lost regarding how we fit into the larger weaving of humanity. I have often heard the words, "Blood doesn't make family." This is true—there are many ways to create a family—but there is something vital for many people about being able to access their genealogical heritage, even when they don't have contact with genealogical family.

Mirror of Connection

In my own scenarios of searching, I used several magical tools but one, a black mirror in a frame that serves as a portal of sorts, has become an important tool for me. This Mirror of Connection is instrumental in helping me to reach out and make connections, and it eases my heart to be able to do so without knowing the names of those I seek. Before starting every research session, I light a candle and use the mirror for gazing and reflecting, and to send and receive messages to and from the ancestors whose identity I am working to discover.

Materials:
> *A stand-alone frame with glass in your choice of style*
> *and size (I used an ornate 5x7 frame)*
> *Black spray paint, glossy*

Instructions:
Carefully remove the glass from the frame, clean it with glass cleaner, let it dry thoroughly. Shake the can of spray paint to mix. Just prior to spraying the paint, exhale your breath very softly on the side of the glass you mean to paint, then say these words:

> *Bless my hands as they do this work, and bless this mirror, that it may serve as a connection between the present and the past, between what is to come and what has gone, between me and those from whose blood I descend. Only that which serves the highest good for all is permitted to come through this portal, and only when it is opened by me.*

Lightly mist the glass several times with the spray paint until the glass is fully obscured and no light shines through. Let it dry, then reassemble the glass and frame with the painted side to the back of the frame.

Keep in mind that it is imperative to work responsibly. Be sure to clearly define the boundaries of your mirror and what is allowed to pass through. Because I created my mirror to be a two-way connection, I am very strict with its use. Here are my basic and non-negotiable rules:

- Always start each mirror session in a way
  that indicates it's time to open.

- Always end each mirror session in a way
  that indicates it's time to close.

- Cleanse the area before and after use with
  a clearing spray of choice.

- When not in use, keep the mirror covered with a
  cloth, or put it away in a drawer or box.

Good magical hygiene is very important with any object that is used to facilitate connections with the spiritual plane. My experiences have always been excellent, and I believe that's because I don't offer up the opportunity for anything to go awry.

To Open the Mirror of Connection

Cleanse your area with a clearing spray, light your seven-day genealogy work candle, and say these words:

The door is open, the way is clear. I welcome loving messages sent with good intent. I am searching for _____.

Describe your request in detail. For example, I would say, "I am searching for the names of my fifth great-grandparents on my Carroll/O'Heron line." Sit with your mirror and gaze into it. If you're so inclined, burn incense, or fill the airspace with background music. Picture in your mind's eye your family tree and the areas where there is missing information. Keep your journal handy and write down anything that comes to mind, no matter how random it may seem.

When you are finished with the mirror, be sure to close the session. Snuff the candle and say these words:

The door is now closed. Thank you for your guidance, and farewell for now.

Cover the mirror with a cloth or put it away in a drawer or box. Cleanse the area with a clearing spray.

> Add a cleansed bloodstone to your genealogy toolbox and use it to represent yourself, your genealogical family of origin, or both during genealogy work. Set it near your Mirror of Connection when it is open and you are seeking information.

5

Three Trees

Call it a clan, call it a network, call it a tribe, call it a family.
Whatever you call it, whoever you are, you need one.

—Jane Howard

How well do you know your family tree? This is the second question I ask any client who comes to me for help with their genealogy pursuits. Most people are familiar with the name and date demographics of their closest relatives: mother, father, siblings. They're mostly familiar with info about their grandparents. Sometimes, just as I was, they're much more knowledgeable about one side of their family. I see a sharp drop-off of knowledge when it comes to great-grandparents, especially as it relates to the family (maiden) surname of the women.

Let's test your knowledge about your genealogical family tree of origin. Light your genealogy work candle, add your clear quartz palm stone and bloodstone crystals to the space. You may want to open your Mirror of Connection for this exercise, to see if your subconscious might be reminded of things you've been told and have since forgotten. Start with yourself and, using memory only, and without referring to any notes or research, create a four-generation family tree to the best of your ability. Be sure to use the pre-marriage surname for your female ancestors. If you know dates of birth, marriage, and death, add them. If you use your Mirror, be sure to close the session once you're done filling in the tree. Here is an example of how you should arrange the people in your tree. It doesn't have to be artistic or perfectly aligned, the important bit is to see what you know without prompts.

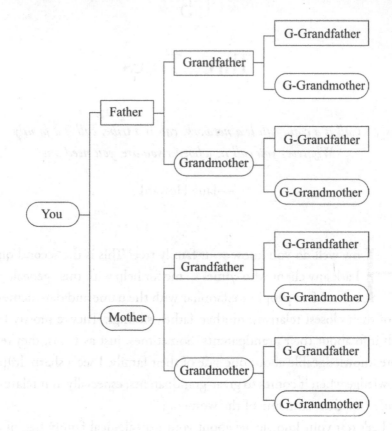

How did you do? Did you know the pre-marriage surname of your most recent female ancestors? How about dates and locations of birth? Marriage dates? These are the demographics that get lost in the passing of time and, if we can access the information, are important to record for posterity and ease in future research. For some of you, the only name on the tree will be your own. For others, it may be too painful to write the names of people from whom you've been disconnected for any number of reasons. For you especially, there are trees other than a bloodline-based genealogical tree you can construct that will give you a sense of connection and belonging.

Many people tend to think of their tree as being a closed system, a sort of "this is my tree and that is your tree" mindset. Trees are viewed from a strictly personal perspective, and the connecting doorway to the larger cosmic tree stays closed. There is much talk among magical folk of feeling spiritually connected, but DNA testing, and its representation of we in the physical, seems to manifest a possessiveness of sorts. Those with whom we are most closely connected genetically are also the ones with whom we share very few unknown genetic associations. However, it's likely that more than one set of your third great-grandparents have many lines of descendants other than yours. These more distant connections serve as a reminder to us that our individual family trees are all part of a vast forest with intertwining roots that attach and connect in many ways, most of which we will likely never know. We are all a tiny part of a great cosmic weaving, one that shifts continuously as new lives come in and old lives go out.

When people consider a family tree, they typically think of their genealogical family of origin, or the people from whom they immediately descend—parents, grandparents, great-grandparents. As genealogy has become more popular in the last decade or so, especially with the advent of DNA testing, knowledge and acceptance of what constitutes family is beginning to evolve. There are many ways to define a family. What isn't so easy is coming to a consensus about how to document family. In the typical genealogical way, our family tree reflects our genetic parents and their direct ancestors. What happens to the tree for the child who is adopted? What tree is there for a person who is removed from their genealogical family and has instead created a family connected by bond instead of blood? The married gay couple? The person with an unknown donor parent, by either egg or sperm, or both? It can get complicated quickly, which is why I love the thought of each of us possessing three trees: lineage, inheritance, and influence. They can each stand alone or be subsets of each other. They offer ways for each person to have a tree that can be researched and that is meaningful and filled with important connections that allow us to be rooted.

The Tree of Lineage

This family tree is very straightforward. In short, it's the pedigree tree that shows our direct genealogical ancestors on every line, going back as far as we can take it with sourced research. This is the tree that shows the big picture of all our ancestral lines. It is also the one that most often presents problems for people who fall outside the parameters that dictate how we enter information into the tree. Adopted people, for example, often don't have access to the information that tells them of their genealogical lineage. Those who uncover family secrets can lose parts of this tree and will need to research to refill those sections. Those descended from enslaved persons may not be able to find any information on some ancestors from before the 1870 census. What is absolute, however, is that we each have one of these trees, even if the information contained within it is unknown to us. There are a few fortunate individuals for whom this tree is very full and overflowing, with documentation to support the additions to it. Those people are rare! Most, like me, have great success on some well-documented lines but, on others, can't get past a certain person. (This is called a brick wall.) Others have no information at all.

On the facing page is an example of my own Tree of Lineage, five generations (counting me as the first generation), current as of this writing. You can see it's full back to my great-great-grandparents. It has taken me many years to get it to this point, mainly because DNA testing uncovered family secrets that took off two major branches and I had to do a lot of work to rebuild them. Beyond that fifth generation, however, I begin to have gaps. I have not yet found the documentation that allows me to firmly place my paternal great-great-grandparents James and Cecelia back to Ireland where, according to information found in newspaper articles and census records, it is presumed that they were born. I have only a guess as to Cecelia's father's name. He is listed as "Patrick O'Heron" in her obituary and as "Michael O'Heron" on her death certificate. I have seen no name yet for her mother. I know almost nothing about James other than he died about thirty-five years before Cecelia. I can find no documentation of Mathilde's father other than

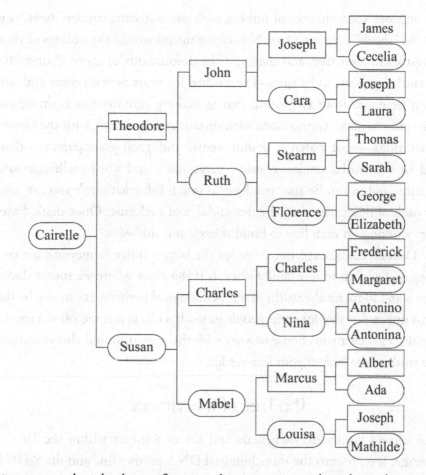

his name on her death certificate, and in one census that also indicates he was born in France around 1808. If I do have that Native American ancestry that I was told I have by the Navajo healer, it's likely on Mathilde's husband Joseph's line, or possibly Albert's mother, both of which are also persistent brick wall lines for me.

The Tree of Lineage is your easiest way to connect with ancestors from the near and distant past. If you want to connect your tree to those of others you should have, at minimum, an accessible and public online tree that is filled in back to the level of your great-grandparents, with the family surname for the women, and dates of birth, marriage, and death included.

To improve your chances of linking with more distant cousins' trees, you should "shrub" your own tree. Shrubbing means to add the siblings of your ancestors to your tree, and then add the descendants of those siblings. It's an endless process to be sure—I've worked for years now on mine and will never be done!—but I've found that in making sure my tree is shrubbed, I am able to make connections with distant cousins. Start with the closest generations—your parents, grandparents, and great-grandparents—then add in the aunts, uncles, cousins, great-aunts and great-uncles, second cousins, and so on. Be sure you have as much information as you can find for each of them regarding the descendants of each line. Once that's done, start working on each line to build it back and sideways.

Overall, the lineage tree provides the largest outer framework for creating and adding to our family story. It is the place where we source documents and shore up the truths of our genealogical heritage. It can also be the most uncomfortable for some people to work with, as it is too often a source of pain. However you choose to work with this tree, it should always contain the truth to the best of your knowledge.

The Tree of Inheritance

This second family tree is genetic and sits as a subset within the Tree of Lineage. It represents the mitochondrial DNA mother line and the Y-DNA father line, as well as the autosomal DNA we inherit from some, but not all, of our ancestors. This concept of genetic inheritance only from certain ancestors confuses some people, as they believe they have physical autosomal DNA within them from every single ancestor in their tree. This is not the case. While we do descend from all our ancestors, we don't carry physical, measurable, autosomal DNA from every single one of them. For example, I am related to a paternal eighth great-grandmother because I descend from a straight line that extends from her to myself. However, over the generations of recombining autosomal DNA, the bits of her that were passed down had all disappeared by the time my genetics were paired up from my mother and father. Well, it's disappeared as much as I'm able to tell from my tested DNA. There are limitations to what information DNA results can provide to me, and it may just be that I haven't found a cousin who also shares DNA from this grandmother that would rule her in as a genetic ancestor (as opposed to a genealogical ancestor).

On page 54 is an example of a Tree of Inheritance.

Of course, this is not how it will be exactly for each person, as our inheritance patterns are random and will not be the same. The shaded areas on the tree represent ancestors from whom there is inheritance of the physical form of autosomal DNA. The ones not shaded represent ancestors from whom there is no inheritance of any physical DNA and who are instead represented within the aura as energetic DNA, which is not measurable by scientific methods. Again, this does not mean we don't descend from the ancestors from whom we carry no physical DNA—we absolutely do. What it does mean is, during the generations between them and us, their DNA simply didn't make it through the multiple tumbles of autosomal DNA that mixes and recombines every time a new generation is created. Of note, this inheritance from more distant ancestors is not immediately apparent with a DNA test. It takes a lot of research using DNA test results to begin the process of adding ancestors beyond our great-great-grandparents to the Tree of Inheritance. This is typically the least favorite tree for most people to work on and fill in, mainly because it can be difficult to do, and it requires a lot of research time and intensive work with genetic genealogy results from DNA testing.

You don't have to fill in this tree. What is most important is that you know this tree exists, and that you have an awareness that you don't carry the physical autosomal DNA of every single one of your ancestors. Some people find that they're very connected to certain ancestors in their Tree of Inheritance. There are others to which you may really feel no connection at all. How are you able to determine which ancestors fall within the Tree of Inheritance? One way is cousin matches!

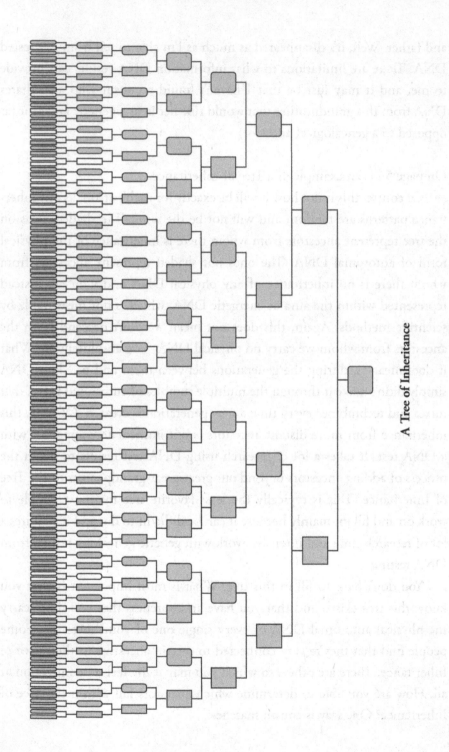

A Tree of Inheritance

Here is an example:

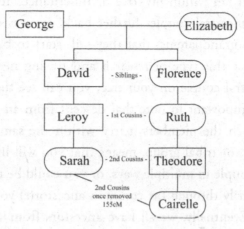

George — Elizabeth

David - Siblings - Florence

Leroy - 1st Cousins - Ruth

Sarah - 2nd Cousins - Theodore

2nd Cousins
once removed
155cM

Cairelle

Shared autosomal DNA is measured in centimorgans, abbreviated as cM. The higher the number, the more you share, and the more closely you're related. (See chapter 7—Autosomal DNA: The Cloak.) My results on Ancestry tell me I share 155 cM of DNA with Sarah, which puts us roughly in the Second/Third Cousin category of relationships. When I look at her online tree, I see a familiar couple—George and Elizabeth—who are two of her great-grandparents. In my own tree, George and Elizabeth are two of my great-great-grandparents, they are parents to my great-grandmother Florence. This tells me two things: Sarah and I are a generation apart and we are second cousins, once removed and, when I follow her ancestral line on her tree, and I then follow mine, I see that we connect at one shared point to the common set of ancestors, George and Elizabeth. This doesn't 100 percent mean that we are only related through this set of grandparents but, with research completed to rule out other ways to be related, I feel fairly assured that this couple is our genetic connection, our "most recent common ancestors" (MRCA). To shore up my theory, I have also confirmed that we both have DNA matches to other people who also trace back to this couple. With the information obtained from a combination of traditional research and shared DNA matches, I can place George and Elizabeth on my Tree of Inheritance.

I fully expected, due to the closeness to me of this ancestral couple, that they would fall within my Tree of Inheritance. You will find, when working with ancestral couples further back, even as close as the great-great-great (3x) grandparents, that they will start to be more difficult to confirm. Because this type of research and tracing needs to be repeated for every ancestral couple on your tree, you can see that it takes a lot of time. It's also important to note that descent from an endogamous population, in which the members marry within the same ethnic, cultural, social, religious, or tribal group, means that you will likely descend from one ancestral couple in multiple ways, or you could be related to someone but not necessarily through the common ancestor(s) you think you share, but another. (Eventually, we all have ancestors from whom we descend in multiple ways.) Another consideration is known as "pedigree collapse" which happens when an ancestral individual or, more typically, an ancestral couple, occupies two or more grandparent spaces in the family tree. You might share this individual or couple with another person, but not on the same line of descent. It can get complicated quickly. Thankfully there are various methods, and genealogy calculators and programs, that can help you figure things out and get them sorted. This is also where genealogy education comes into play. Creating a four-generation tree is easy when you have access to the information, and you can be assured if all the paternity/maternity connections are intact, that you will share DNA with every person on that tree. It's when we begin to move further back with research that we start to see gaps.

What about the ancestors who fall into these gaps, whose autosomal DNA we didn't physically inherit? They are still our ancestors, of course, and I believe we continue to carry them with us, along with access to their knowledge and wisdom, in the form of energetic DNA, which resides within our aura. While the Tree of Inheritance contains only the ancestors with whom we share a genetic connection, remember that the Tree of Lineage encompasses all of our genealogical ancestors, no matter whether their DNA is present within us physically or energetically.

The Tree of Influence

The third type of family tree is the Tree of Influence. This tree is reserved for the people in your life who have had a profoundly positive effect on you in some way. Not everyone has a biological child, but everyone can be a positive influence in a child's life, and thus can become an ancestor of influence. We also influence the lives of others, hopefully in a good way, and that places us on their list of influential family. The Tree of Influence can stand alone as the singular tree with which you identify solely, or it can be another subset of the Tree of Lineage, like the Tree of Inheritance. Typically, the Tree of Influence will be less structured and more casual, with people generally fitting into, or next to, the spots typically reserved for mother, father, sibling, cousin, or grandparent.

What does it mean to have an ancestor of influence? I'll share an example of two of my own. One person on my Tree of Influence is my best friend, Christine. I have biological sisters, one with whom I very am close, and I also put Christine in the "sister" category as that's how I identify her in my life. She is like a sister to me. My children have known her for most of their lives and I've known hers, and my grandchildren call her Aunt Christine. Her influence in my life has been profound, from her sage advice (well, maybe not always so sage, but still . . .) to her constant presence when I had need of support. She is always on the other end of the phone when I call. Most importantly, we laugh. A lot! I cannot imagine my life without her in it.

Another person on my Tree of Influence sits in a position next to my father. My dad and mom divorced when I was three years old. Due to certain circumstances, between the ages of four and seven, I lived with my father and a stepmother near Washington, DC. I remember riding with my dad in the car, us singing along to the radio, while he pointed out interesting sights and told me about them. He was a fun, friendly, and brilliant man with an aptitude for math and a deep love of history and politics. He also struggled with alcoholism and wasn't always the best father he could've been. After the age of seven, and after I returned home to New Orleans, I saw him exactly five times before he died when I was forty-seven and he was seventy. He's been gone since December 2014, and I wonder how different things might've been for me if I'd had my father in my day-to-day life while growing up. He loved me dearly, I know this without a doubt, but adult me has also wrestled with the hurt and loss of his absence. Children, however, are quite resilient, and I was no different. During my years up north, I "met" Fred Rogers one morning when I came across the children's show *Mr. Roger's Neighborhood*. Mr. Rogers was soft-spoken, gentle, and loving; he made me feel like I mattered. After returning to New Orleans, and with the loss of my father in my everyday life, Fred Rogers somehow became my "real" father in my little girl mind. I was devastated whenever I missed a show. Of course, I ultimately recognized and accepted that he was a TV personality and not my father, but his lessons of kindness, compassion, and acceptance have resonated with me through the years. Through the television medium, he became an important and influential person in my life.

Some children, like me, grow up without the presence of one of their parents. Not all children are fortunate enough that their primary caregiving parent will partner with a person who leads by example, who provides the necessities for a stable life, and who shows genuine love and affection for a child that isn't genetically theirs. Multiple studies have shown the negative effect this lack of one parent has on self-esteem, drug and alcohol use, and lifetime earning potential, among other things. In my own case, I substituted Fred Rogers in my child mind as a father figure. His influence has remained with me throughout my life so far, to the point that I tell myself, "Look for the helpers!" whenever something terrible happens (like Hurricane Katrina). I cried bitter tears when he died, and he holds a place of honor on my ancestor altar. He is a wonderful example of a person who sits on a branch of my Tree of Influence.

Other people may come from circumstances in which they've chosen to remove themselves fully from the sphere of their genealogical family, or they were expelled, and have discovered the love and support of people who may not be genetically related to them. This happens far too often with LGBTQIA+ people, it has happened with young unwed mothers, with those who do not toe a religious line, and for many others for different reasons. In light of their often-total disconnection from genealogical family, adoptees often have a very full Tree of Influence. While I do believe it's important to have a multi-generational knowledge of one's genealogical family history, if even for just a medical history, it's just as important to document the people who are chosen family.

The Tree of Influence is typically an odd shape, perhaps it resembles a shrub, or it just has a couple of branches. It can look awkward or uneven. That's okay. What's important is that we realize how much this tree matters. Ancestral healing is an integral part of genealogy magic, and the Tree of Influence helps to work with that healing energy. It brings us to a place of belonging, connects us with the larger stream of consciousness that flows through us all, and reminds us that we are part of a grander scheme than we find in our immediate genealogical family.

For my own Tree of Influence, I consider it to be a subset of my Tree of Lineage, like my Tree of Inheritance.

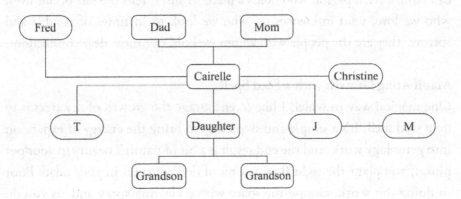

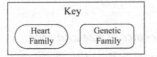

In this abbreviated example of my tree, I have placed my family of influence within ovals, and my lineage family in rectangles. The key explains the symbols, thus anyone else who sees the tree can know that these circled people, while not necessarily genetically related, are very important to me and that I consider them to be as much a part of my family as my genealogical relatives. Fred Rogers takes on a "heart father" spot, and Christine has been added to me as a "heart sister." My daughter has had a friend, T, since early childhood, and I love her dearly. She calls me "Mama Deuce." She is on my tree as a "heart daughter." There are also two young men in my life, J and M, that have been important to me since their early childhood, my "heart sons."

The Tree of Influence's beauty lies in its ability to stretch beyond the confines of genealogical and genetic family. I believe it to be the most accurate tree to represent our family story, as it can hold both genealogical and genetic family, and it expands beautifully to hold those we have chosen to call family. Each person who holds a place within it tells the tale of our lives, who we love, who influences us, who we look to in times of trouble and sorrow. They are the people with whom we hold our most dear connections.

Manifesting Growth with a Seed Spell

One magical way in which I like to encourage the growth of my trees is to do a seed spell. It's a simple and sweet way to bring the energy of expansion into genealogy work, and the end result is a bit of nature's beauty in your pot plus, if you plant the right flower, a bit of deliciousness in your salad! Prior to doing this work, cleanse the space with a clearing spray and, as you do this work, keep the intention in mind that your tree will flourish and grow right along with the seeds.

Materials:

A pot in which to put seeds and soil, your choice of size and style
A bit of gravel for the inside base of the pot, to assist with drainage
Soil that is suitable for nutritionally nurturing and supporting seeds/plants

Seeds of your choice—I prefer to use something quick growing that
    will produce an edible flower, like nasturtium or cornflower
A piece of compostable paper on which you can
    write and then bury, and a pen
Water

Instructions:

Put the gravel in the bottom of the pot and add soil until the pot is half full.

On the piece of compostable paper, write details about the tree you wish to grow on the piece of paper. For example, I'd say, "I want to grow my Tree of Lineage with information about my father's paternal line," or "I want to know the name of Louis's parents so I can grow that branch on my Tree of Inheritance." Be specific, and word it in any way you choose. I tend to be very direct when writing, others like to rhyme and be a bit more expressive.

Place the paper in the pot and cover with soil until the pot is about 3/4 full.

Add a few of the seeds and cover them with 1/4 inch of soil.

Water the soil until it is saturated, and place in a sunny windowsill. From then on, water according to the instructions on the seed packet. Each time you water, envision the healthy growth of your plants and, along with that, the growth of your tree. You may wish to keep the plant near your workspace.

Keep a "record keeper" clear quartz on your workspace to help connect you to ancestral lines and to amplify your access to information while researching. Place it near your plant to add power to your intention to grow your family tree.

6

Elements of You: DNA

We inherit from our ancestors gifts so often taken for granted. Each of us contains within us this inheritance of soul. We are links between the ages, containing past and present expectations, sacred memories and future promise.

—Edward Sellner, *Soul Making*

Each of us is an amalgamation of smaller pieces that make up a whole. The beauty of our genetics is that we're each a completely unique individual—even identical twins have slight differences. Within the beauty, however, are biological puzzle pieces that can leave people feeling a bit confused. Much like when a house is built and the foundation is laid first to support all the pieces that sit atop it, we should do the same when working with genealogy and magic. To enjoy the deepest experiences and the highest potential, we must first know as much as we can about the genetic basics of our physical body before we move toward integrating it with a magical practice that focuses on it. Reminiscing about Biology 101 isn't everyone's cup of tea, however. To really get a good grasp on blending genealogy with magic, a basic understanding of the elements is necessary. This probably won't be the most exciting thing you'll read today, but it's important, so grab that cup of tea and settle in. Take a while to read through these basics of DNA so that you can more easily maneuver in the world of genetic genealogy and magic and gain a fuller understanding of your place within the world tree.

Simplified Biology

In the human body, the cell is the basic unit of life. We are comprised of trillions of cells, each doing their part to contribute to the harmony and well-being of our whole. Within each cell is a nucleus, also known as the cell's control center, and inside of the nucleus is a genetic material called deoxyribonucleic acid. Most of us know it by its common acronym, DNA, and each DNA molecule is assembled in a very specific way.

DNA (deoxyribonucleic acid) is the double helix that we see so often as a symbol to represent genealogy. It is a "double-stranded" molecule made with two strings of nucleotides. These strings are wrapped around each other in a twisted spiraling fashion, much like a ladder, and are held together in bonded pairs of nucleotides. The DNA acts like an instruction manual and directs the majority of the cell's functions, from its beginning, when its parent cells divide, to its death, when the cell fully ceases to function.

Nucleotides, as millions of smaller pieces strung together, make up a molecule of DNA. You may recall seeing them represented together as the letters A, C, G, and T. Those letters together—ACGT—are an acronym that stands for, respectively, adenine, cytosine, guanine, and thymine. In DNA, adenine pairs with thymine, and cytosine pairs with guanine. Together, AT and CG are known as "base pairs" and they are held together by hydrogen bonds within DNA's spiral.

Genes are a very tiny segment of DNA that, via a "coding region" that acts as a blueprint of sorts, give our cells instructions to perform certain specialized actions, like creating proteins that will help to keep our body healthy. Genes also have different variations, known as alleles, and we inherit these alleles in pairs, one from each parent. Multiple genes work together in ways that are not yet fully understood, but the science is continually evolving.

Chromosomes are created when two DNA molecules intertwine and connect into one double helix structure. Each cell's nucleus has a total of ninety-two molecules that form forty-six double-stranded chromosomes. When one of the forty-six chromosomes connect with another, similar, chromosome, twenty-three different chromosome pairs are created. In every pair, one copy of each chromosome has been inherited from each parent.

In addition to the cell's nucleus and all of its contents mentioned above, there is another structure within the cell that contains its own DNA, an organelle, called a mitochondrion. There are many mitochondria within each cell, and their responsibility is to create the energy our cells need to function. Inside of each mitochondrion are thousands of copies of a very small circular strand of DNA. This particular DNA is inherited only from the mother/XX parent who passes an exact replica of her mitochondrial DNA to all offspring.

Confused yet? It is complicated and also can be a bit difficult to visualize and understand. The important takeaway from this brief lesson is that our bodies are gloriously built, piece by piece, with a near-infinite number of microscopic bits that all come together in a unique way, thanks to our ancestors and the DNA that we inherit from them. Therein lies the magic!

The Five Sacred Elements of You

Each person has four different types of physical DNA: autosomal DNA (atDNA), mitochondrial DNA (mtDNA), X-DNA, and Y-DNA. These types of DNA are inherited on different pathways from each parent and are passed down similarly.

Although it's not found in any mainstream science-based discussions of which I'm aware, magical people are generally familiar with the aura. Within the aura is contained ancient, uninherited ancestral DNA, which is energetic in form.

Each type of DNA has magical and elemental correspondences.

Autosomal DNA

atDNA refers to the chromosome pairs that are found in the nucleus of every cell. Remember from our earlier lesson that we have twenty-three pairs of chromosomes. Twenty-two of these pairs are autosomal DNA (autosomes) and the twenty-third pair is an X/Y DNA combo (sex chromosomes) that designate us as genetically female or male. One copy of each chromosome is inherited from the mother/XX parent, and one copy is inherited from the father/XY parent. A section of atDNA is what is examined with most commercial direct-to-consumer DNA tests. The results reveal information about both maternal and paternal lines. This is the DNA that contributes to the ethnicity estimate found in popular genealogical DNA testing results like Ancestry.

Autosomal DNA corresponds with the Cloak and the element of Air.

Mitochondrial DNA

mtDNA refers to the DNA found inside mitochondria, which are a type of organelle found in almost all complex cells. They are known as the power plants of the cell because they supply an enzyme or, more accurately, a co-enzyme, known as adenosine triphosphate (ATP). This ATP is the source for the chemical energy needed by a cell to perform a wide range of functions. Mitochondrial DNA is passed down on the maternal line from the mother/XX parent to her genetic offspring. Every few thousand years, a small mutation will occur that causes a slight change in the line that continues. These mutations are classed into haplotrees, which are then organized into haplogroups, which are then grouped on a phylogenetic tree, which is like a family tree for mitochondrial DNA. This DNA does not contribute to or show up in the ethnicity estimate result.

Mitochondrial DNA corresponds with the Crown and the element of Fire.

X-DNA

X-DNA is one of the two chromosomes that determine sex. Males have one X chromosome from their mother/XX parent (their other is a Y chromosome from their father/XY parent) and they can derive information about their maternal line from testing. Females have two X chromosomes, one from their mother and one from their father, and they can derive information about both maternal and paternal lines from testing. X-DNA information and matching is included in some autosomal DNA tests, but does not contribute to the ethnicity estimate result.

X-DNA corresponds with the Chalice and the element of Water.

Y-DNA

Also known as Y-chromosome DNA, this is one of the two chromosomes that determine sex, and it stands alone as its own separate DNA test. Males get one Y chromosome from their father/XY parent (their other is an X from their mother/XX parent) and this is passed along directly on the paternal line. Females do not inherit any Y-DNA from their male parent. As with mitochondrial DNA, every few thousand years, a small mutation will occur in a male's Y-DNA that causes a slight change in the line that continues to be passed down. These mutations are classed into haplotrees, which are then organized into haplogroups, which are then grouped on a phylogenetic tree, which is like a family tree for Y-DNA. This DNA does not contribute to or show up in the ethnicity estimate result.

Y-DNA corresponds with the Staff and the element of Earth.

Energetic DNA

This type of DNA is not something you'll find in a science-based DNA discussion. It's energetic in nature, contains the echoes of the near and distant past, and is a compilation of the genetic bits of the ancestors we did not physically inherit. Although we do not carry this DNA in our physical body, it is with us in the form of energy contained within our aura and is a source of genetic memory. This magical, non-scientific DNA cannot be tested and does not show up in genealogical DNA test results.

Energetic DNA corresponds with the Aura and the element of Spirit.

Haplogroups, Haplotrees, and Phylogenetic Trees

Mitochondrial DNA and Y-DNA are categorized into haplogroups. The International Society of Genetic Genealogy (ISOGG) wiki defines a haplogroup as

> *a genetic population group of people who share a common ancestor on the patriline or the matriline. Top-level haplogroups are assigned letters of the alphabet, and deeper refinements consist of additional number and letter combinations. For Y-DNA, a haplogroup may be shown in the long-form nomenclature established by the Y Chromosome Consortium or it may be expressed in a short-form using a deepest-known single nucleotide polymorphism (SNP) . . . Y-chromosome and mitochondrial DNA haplogroups have different haplogroup designations. Haplogroups can reveal deep ancestral origins dating back thousands of years, or with recent full-sequence Y-DNA testing may be relevant to the last few generations.*[7]

Females/XX people have one haplogroup because they have mitochondrial DNA but no Y-DNA. Males/XY people have two haplogroups because they have both mitochondrial DNA and Y-DNA.

- A haplotree is a chart or a diagram that shows the different lineages within a single haplogroup.

- A phylogenetic tree is a chart or a diagram that shows the various top-level haplogroups for mitochondrial DNA and Y-DNA.

For example, I have a mitochondrial haplogroup designation of H1. My H1 is a branch on the haplotree of the larger H haplogroup. The H haplogroup is a branch on the larger phylogenetic tree for mitochondrial DNA that shows how all the haplogroups are related.

---

[7] ISOGG Genetics Glossary: *https://isogg.org*

This is an example of a simple phylogenetic tree for the various mitochon-drial haplogroups. H is one of the branches. My haplogroup, H1, sits on the H branch as one of its twigs. The other branches loosely represent the other haplogroups. (Bigstock)

DNA Testing

We are each uniquely made of genetic snippets passed down to us from the generations that came before us, and the first step in working with genetic genealogy is to do a direct-to-consumer DNA test. Recall that we each have four types of DNA that can be tested. This is done via three different kinds of direct-to-consumer DNA tests: atDNA (includes X-DNA), mtDNA, and Y-DNA. There are several options available. For those just setting out on the path of DNA testing, it can all seem a bit daunting. More details about testing are provided in the upcoming chapters, but here is a brief summary to guide you.

- Ancestry tests atDNA and has the largest database for DNA matching. There is also a large repository of documents, as well as access to DNA match trees, for an additional monthly fee. There are often specials and discounts to be found. This is the first test I recommend for most people.

- 23andMe tests atDNA and also top-level haplogroups for mtDNA for XX and XY people, and Y-DNA for XY people. It also provides some basic health information for an additional fee. If the budget can afford it, I suggest this test in conjunction with Ancestry as a good way to kickstart your genetic genealogy work.

- MyHeritage tests atDNA and its database for matching is growing. This site also allows an upload of raw DNA data that has been downloaded from another site, such as Ancestry. The results are free to view. There is a nominal fee to then use the site's tools to work with uploaded DNA results.

- Family Tree DNA tests atDNA, full sequence mtDNA for XX and XY people, Y-DNA tests from a very basic Y-37 to the full Big-Y 700 for XY people, and also allows an upload of raw DNA data for atDNA. Results are free to view; there is a nominal fee to use the site's tools to work with uploaded atDNA results. If you plan to test mtDNA or Y-DNA, or both, at Family Tree DNA, consider that you might not need to test at 23andMe unless you're someone who is searching for genealogical family.

- Living DNA tests atDNA and gives a top-level haplogroup for mtDNA for XX and XY people, and a top-level haplogroup for Y-DNA for XY people. In my current experience, this test gives the most detailed ethnicity estimate if the tester is of NW European descent. They also offer "Wellness" information and DNA matching.

If you are someone who is searching, it is best to be in every available database for atDNA, as you can never know where other people will choose to test. I also suggest you upload your raw atDNA data to a site called GEDmatch, which is a site that compiles other uploaded data from the various companies. Here you will be able to see matches with people who have tested at other companies and then uploaded their DNA data, and they offer a wide array of tools that can help with comparing your DNA to that of your matches.

Of note, one should always read carefully the terms and conditions of testing on each website, especially in regard to privacy, and be sure they're acceptable to you. Law enforcement and other forensic organizations do use some databases to build trees for their cold cases. They cannot access your personal DNA results and they cannot see your DNA. They only look at DNA matches to their cold cases, and they use that information to construct a tree that will hopefully lead to the solving of a crime or to identify a deceased person who is nameless. I personally have not had any issue with privacy, or any other concerns, over nearly a decade of testing myself and family, and I would be thrilled for my DNA to contribute to the solving of a cold case. However, this is something that only you can decide for yourself.

7

Autosomal DNA: The Cloak

Genes are like the story, and DNA is the language that the story is written in.

—Sam Kean

utosomal DNA, or atDNA for short, refers to the chromosome pairs that are found in the nucleus of every cell. Remember from our earlier lesson that we have twenty-three pairs of chromosomes. Twenty-two of these pairs are autosomal DNA (autosomes) and the twenty-third pair is an XX or XY DNA combo (sex chromosomes) that designate us as genetically female or male. One copy of each chromosome is inherited from the mother/XX parent, and one copy is inherited from the father/XY parent. A section of atDNA is what is examined with most commercial direct-to-consumer DNA tests, and the results reveal information about both maternal and paternal lines. Autosomal DNA is the DNA that is probably most well-known, and it is the kind of DNA that is tested in DNA tests that can be taken by both males and females to estimate ethnicity and to obtain matches to people with whom DNA is shared in varying amounts.

How We Inherit Autosomal DNA

We inherit autosomal DNA in equal portion, approximately 50 percent from each of our parents. Since we inherit only about half of each parents' DNA, this means there's a lot of room for variation. Autosomal DNA is a mover and shaker when it comes to genetic inheritance. With every single conception, a random pattern of autosomal DNA is passed along. While it is statistically possible, it is highly improbable that you share an identical DNA pattern with someone else. Identical twins are the exception, of course. Even full siblings, including fraternal twins, can have vastly different inheritance patterns of autosomal DNA. Recombination is responsible for these differences. Consider your parents' DNA contributions to you to be like the ping-pong balls in a lottery. They each have one hundred ping-pong balls to give you, but the limit to their contribution can be only fifty ping-pong balls. Like a lottery, a random 50 percent of their DNA is going to be passed to you, while another random 50 percent may be passed to any other genetic offspring. This is why siblings can look so different and also have different DNA matches than their siblings. When you consider that your own parents' DNA is also a random combination of their own parents, and the ancestors before them, you can see how there's a near-endless combination of genetics that can be passed along!

We can use a simple math problem to serve as an easy way to think about it:

$$50 + 50 = 100$$

Let's apply the lottery analogy to that math problem:

50 ping-pong balls (autosomal DNA) from Mom/XX parent

+

50 ping-pong balls (autosomal DNA) from Dad/XY parent

=

100 ping-pong balls—100 percent of autosomal DNA

We each need one hundred ping-pong balls of autosomal DNA in total to create our complete autosomal DNA inheritance. We get fifty from each parent. Our mother/XX parent has one hundred individual ping-pong balls to give us, but we can take only fifty from her, so what we get from her is completely randomized, much like a lottery drawing of fifty ping-pong balls out of one hundred. Our father/XY parent also has one hundred individual ping-pong balls to give us, but, again, we can take only fifty and what we get is also randomized like a lottery drawing in which we get fifty ping-pong balls out of one hundred.

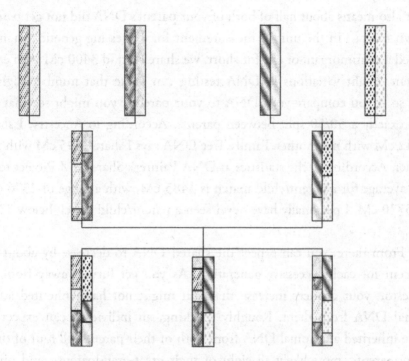

This is a simplified chart to show how autosomal inheritance might look in a set of siblings. One thing to keep in mind is that, for demonstration purposes, the grandparents are shown as one pattern, but in reality, every ancestor each has their own unique variation of autosomal DNA. Consider that, and perhaps you can imagine how DNA from our more distant ancestors can easily get lost in the generational shuffle.

How Much Autosomal DNA Do We Inherit?

Each person inherits around 50 percent of their autosomal DNA from their parents. This means you share half your genome, your complete set of genes, with your mother/XX parent and half with your father/XY parent. Because you inherited only about half of each parent's autosomal DNA, that also means about half of both of your parent's DNA did not get passed down to you. In the unit of measurement for expressing genetic distance, called a centimorgan, or cM for short, we share around 3400 cM with each parent. Slight variations in DNA testing can make that number slightly off, so if you compare your DNA to your parents, you might see that it's not exactly a 50/50 split between parents. According to Ancestry, I share 3442 cM with my mother. Family Tree DNA says I share 3595 cM with my father. According to the statistics at DNA Painter's Shared cM Project tool, the average for a parent/child match is 3485 cM, with a range of 2376 cM to 3720 cM. I personally have never seen a parent/child match below 3300 cM.

From there, you can expect the shared DNA to decrease by about 50 percent for each successive generation. As you get further away from an ancestor, your chances increase that you might not have inherited autosomal DNA from them. Roughly speaking, an individual can expect to have inherited autosomal DNA from both of their parents, all four of their grandparents, most likely all eight of their great-grandparents, and probably all sixteen of their great-great-grandparents, although at those odds, there's a chance you won't. From that point, it gets dicey. An individual can likely expect to have inherited autosomal DNA from most of their third great-grandparents, but it's not a given. An individual might have inherited DNA from some of their fifth to eighth great-grandparents, but again, not a given. This is how ancestors are lost from our Tree of Inheritance but remain in our Tree of Lineage. We descend from all of them but have not inherited autosomal DNA from all of them.

Let's look at this from another perspective. Here's how the percentage of autosomal DNA inheritance breaks down by generation:

Generation:	Percent DNA Inherited
Parent	50%
Grandparent	25%
Great-Grandparent	12.5%
GG-Grandparent	6.25%
GGG-Grandparent	3.125%

The percentages continue to decrease from there, and you can see how, statistically, we'll eventually start to lose those ancestors I mentioned earlier, meaning we won't inherit any of their autosomal DNA. This is the technical breakdown, however. The reality is a bit different, and less structured. The easiest example to share is that between grandparents and grandchildren. We are technically supposed to inherit 25 percent of our autosomal DNA from each grandparent, as indicated above. Instead, the autosomal DNA inheritance from grandparents might look like this for two siblings who share both parents:

Grandchild 1 Inherited DNA and Grandchild 2 Inherited DNA

	Grandchild 1	Grandchild 2
Maternal Grandma 1	26%	27%
Maternal Grandpa 2	24%	23%
Paternal Grandma 3	28%	21%
Paternal Grandpa 4	22%	29%

So, while each grandchild inherits autosomal DNA from each of their grandparents, they do so in different percentages. Why? Recombination! It happens randomly during meiosis, which is defined as "the stage in which sperm and egg cells are formed. It is during this process that the autosomal chromosomes recombine and mutations occur."[8] Remember, even though we each get 50 percent of our autosomal DNA from our parents, an effect

---

[8] ISOGG Genetics Glossary: *https://isogg.org*

of recombination means each child doesn't get the same 50 percent. Also, due to recombination, our parents aren't going to give us an exact 25 percent split of DNA from their own parents. You can see that grandchild number one got 26 percent of their maternal grandmother's DNA but grandchild number two got 27 percent. The difference is more striking with the inherited autosomal DNA from the paternal grandparents. This pattern of random decrease, until there's statistically none left to inherit, continues as each new generation has their own offspring.

Let's look at how multiple descendants will inherit autosomal DNA differently in another way. Say you're building out an extensive family tree and come across a fourth cousin that shares the same ancestor. You discover that each of you has done a DNA test, however, you don't share any autosomal DNA. Does that mean you didn't inherit any autosomal DNA from the shared ggg-grandparent? Not necessarily. While it could appear that you didn't inherit autosomal DNA from the shared ggg-grandparent, maybe neither of you did (statistically unlikely but not impossible). However, because around 30 percent of fourth cousins don't share any autosomal DNA at all, even though they descend from a common ancestor, what it probably means is that you and your non-matching fourth cousin just didn't inherit the same segments of autosomal DNA, not necessarily that you don't each have DNA from that ancestor. Therefore, it's important to not draw conclusions about relationships, or potential breaks in a genetic family line, with limited information.

Here is a summary of a statistics exercise that was done by using coin flips to ascertain the statistical chance of not inheriting autosomal DNA from the four generations of grandparents closest to you:

Chances of no autosomal DNA inheritance from one grandparent: 1 in 8.4 million

Chances of no autosomal DNA inheritance from one great-grandparent: 1 in 4096

*Chances of no autosomal DNA inheritance
from one great-great-grandparent: 1 in 64*

*Chances of no autosomal DNA inheritance from
one great-great-great-grandparent: 1 in 8*[9]

In short, because recombination occurs in every generation, there is a decreasing amount of shared DNA between an ancestor and their descendants as the number of generations increases between them. You may hear this referred to as an ancestor's autosomal DNA being washed out as successive generations are born.

Autosomal DNA Test Results

One of the hardest, and most exciting, parts of autosomal DNA testing for me is waiting for the results! I am always eager to see how the ethnicity estimate will look, and very interested in who's in the matches, especially for clients who are searching. While it's thrilling to get results from DNA testing, it can be confusing and overwhelming for people who are not familiar with how to look at them and interpret what is seen. I have a set way now that I look at DNA testing results.

First, go ahead and look at the ethnicity estimate. Remember, however, that it is an estimate. I cannot stress this strongly enough. You are not going to see everything you want to see here, and you might see some things you don't want to see, so keep in mind that this estimate is just that. It's fun, and it can offer hints as to the places from where our ancestors came from, but in the larger scheme of genealogy, it cannot be considered proof of anything, really. Ethnicity estimates are generally only valid at the continental level.

I love ethnicity estimates, especially comparing them with parents and siblings if that is an option. Don't let the inconsistencies turn you off of DNA testing. These estimates are meant to provide a glimpse into the

---

[9] From "Ask a Geneticist" at *The Tech Interactive* blog: *https://genetics.thetech.org*

general categories into which we might fall in terms of who our people were, back in time. It is also worthy of remembering that we tend to think of places within modern borders. This is a mistake. It will serve a lot of people if they'd give themselves a crash course in the history of borders around the world. Also, our ancestors traveled! It takes only one traveling man to create and leave behind a large group of descendants along his path. It takes only one woman to birth her children in a place far from where her own parents were born, lived, and died.

One complaint I hear a lot is how ethnicity estimates can't be right because they look so different between siblings. I have tested all my siblings, save one. Of all of them, I have the most in common with my full sibling, with whom I share both parents. This is not surprising because we each got 50 percent of our DNA from the same two people. I also know my half siblings' mother is a first generation American with nearly 100 percent Eastern European ancestry and I do not have very much of that in my mother's known recent ancestry. It's easy for me to see the fairly clear split in our maternal ancestry. However, between my full sister and I, there are a lot of similarities, but also some significant differences, as shown here.

Cairelle		Kelly	
England & NW Europe	41%	Ireland	24%
Wales	12%	England & NW Europe	21%
Ireland	11%	Germanic Europe	16%
Southern Italy	9%	Sweden & Denmark	11%
Norway	8%	Wales	9%
Scotland	6%	France	7%
Sweden & Denmark	5%	Norway	5%
France	3%	Scotland	4%
Germanic Europe	3%	Levant	2%
Northern Africa	1%	Greece & Albania	1%
Northern Italy	1%		

The similarities between us are fairly evident to me, and the differences make sense with what I know of our shared genealogical heritage. I have seen other sibling results that show much bigger differences but that still fall within the realm of normal. Again, ethnicity estimates are fun, and can provide broad clues about our roots. An important point to remember is that the ethnicity estimate should never be used to determine whether or not two people are related. Save that for the shared DNA!

Autosomal DNA Matches

One of the most confusing aspects of receiving DNA results is figuring out who's who. For those who are not adopted or searching, the top matches are usually easy to identify and consist of relatives well-known, or at least somewhat familiar, to us. Once you scroll down the page, however, people unknown to you are going to start showing up. One of the most fun parts of genealogy for me is figuring out how I am related to these matches.

How the matches are categorized can also be puzzling. Because there can be multiple kinds of relationships that share a similar amount of DNA, most testing websites default to a common category and add information about other options. The expectation is that people will do their own research and come to the relationship conclusion that is correct for their scenario. This can be somewhat confusing for people, like adoptees, who are searching for one or more genetic parents.

While the recombination of autosomal DNA is random and has no set pattern, the amount of DNA we share with certain relatives is consistent within a range. No matter your ethnicity or who you believe your genetic parents to be, you will always be related in some way to a person with whom you share DNA. (The exception is small segments which randomly occur just because we're all human.) The amount of shared autosomal DNA can narrow down the way you're related to someone, but it can also be a bit confusing when you're looking at DNA match results on your testing company's platform.

Here's a chart from the DNA Painter website's Shared cM Project tool that shows the average autosomal DNA shared for each relationship, along with a range.

The Shared cM Project – Version 4.0 (March 2020)

Blaine T. Bettinger
www.TheGeneticGenealogist.com
CC 4.0 Attribution License

How to read this chart:

Aunt/Uncle	← Relationship
1741	← Average
1201 – 2282	← Range (min–max)

Direct line (ancestors / descendants)

Relationship	Average	Range
Great-Grandparent	887	485 – 1486
Grandparent	1754	984 – 2462
Parent	3485	2376 – 3720
SELF		
Child	3487	2376 – 3720
Grandchild	1754	984 – 2462
Great-Grandchild	887	485 – 1486

Siblings and their descendants

Relationship	Average	Range
Sibling	2613	1613 – 3488
Half-Sibling	1759	1160 – 2436
Niece/Nephew	1740	1201 – 2282
Half Niece/Nephew	871	492 – 1315
Great-Niece/Nephew	850	330 – 1467
Half Great Niece/Nephew	431	184 – 668
Great-Great Niece/Nephew	420	186 – 713
Half GG Niece/Nephew	208	103 – 284

Aunt/Uncle line

Relationship	Average	Range
Aunt/Uncle	1741	1201 – 2282
Half Aunt/Uncle	871	492 – 1315
1C	866	396 – 1397
Half 1C	449	156 – 979
1C1R	433	102 – 980
Half 1C1R	224	62 – 469
1C2R	221	33 – 471
Half 1C2R	125	16 – 269
1C3R	117	25 – 238
Half 1C3R	60	0 – 120

Great-Aunt/Uncle line

Relationship	Average	Range
Great Aunt/Uncle	850	330 – 1467
Half Great-Aunt/Uncle	431	184 – 668
1C1R	433	102 – 980
2C	229	41 – 592
Half 2C	120	10 – 325
2C1R	122	14 – 353
Half 2C1R	66	0 – 190
2C2R	71	0 – 244
Half 2C2R	48	0 – 144
2C3R	51	0 – 154
Half 2C3R	27	0 – 78

Great-Great-Grandparent / Great-Great Aunt/Uncle line

Relationship	Average	Range
Great-Great Aunt/Uncle	420	186 – 713
1C2R	221	33 – 471
2C1R	122	14 – 353
3C	73	0 – 234
Half 3C	48	0 – 168
3C1R	48	0 – 192
Half 3C1R	37	0 – 139
3C2R	36	0 – 166
Half 3C2R	27	0 – 78
3C3R	27	0 – 98
Half 3C3R	60	0 – 120

Great-Great-Great-Grandparent / GGG-Aunt/Uncle line

Relationship	Average	Range
1C3R	117	25 – 238
2C2R	71	0 – 244
3C1R	48	0 – 192
4C	35	0 – 139
4C1R	28	0 – 126
4C2R	22	0 – 93
4C3R	19	0 – 60

GGGG-Aunt/Uncle line

Relationship	Average	Range
2C3R	51	0 – 154
3C2R	36	0 – 166
4C1R	28	0 – 126
5C	25	0 – 117
5C1R	21	0 – 80
5C2R	18	0 – 65
5C3R	13	0 – 30

Other Relationships

Relationship	Average	Range
6C	18	0 – 71
6C1R	15	0 – 56
6C2R	13	0 – 45
7C	14	0 – 57
7C1R	12	0 – 50
7C2R		
8C	11	0 – 42

Minimum was automatically set to 0 cM for relationships more distant than Half 2C, and averages were determined only for submissions in which DNA was shared

Take your time and study the chart. You can see that there are relationships that share a similar amount of autosomal DNA, like half aunt/uncle, 1C (first cousin), and great-grandchild. The variations in potential relationships within a similar range of shared autosomal DNA can certainly cause confusion. Because you can be related to a DNA match in more than one way, the testing company cannot know how to classify your relationship, so they default to a "Cousin" category.

For example, if you have a DNA match with whom you shared 852 cM, the testing company will default to the 1st—2nd Cousin label to describe how this person is related to you. However, it could be any one of these: Great-Grandparent, Great-Aunt/Uncle, Half Aunt/Uncle, Cousin (1C), Half Niece/Nephew, Great-Niece/Nephew, Great-Grandchild. The lesson? Other than a parent/child match, do not take the label assigned as the true relationship! You must look at the shared DNA amount, determine the various potential relationships, and research. I cannot stress this enough. Unless you know the person and are sure about how the person is related to you, a relationship cannot be assigned without research.

Let's look at this one more time. Beth shares 1793 cM (around 26 percent) with Nate and shares 1839 cM (again around 26 percent) with Brian. Without access to her family tree or knowledge of her family, I cannot tell exactly how they are related to her. Ancestry will class them as Close Family—1st Cousin but that doesn't make things very clear. It is only by looking at her tree that I can see Nate is her grandson and Brian is her paternal half-brother—they share a father but have different mothers. Without a family tree, I would have to engage in researching shared matches to try and determine the relationship.

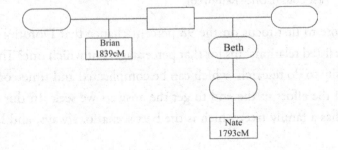

As an example of a confusing relationship designation by the testing company compounded by the complication of an unknown genealogical tree due to adoption, I'll use the DNA match between Cindy, an adoptee, and Dorothy, one of Cindy's DNA matches. Cindy was a client who came to me for help with discovering her genealogical family of origin. I now know the relationship between Cindy and Dorothy, but I'll go through the highlights of how I determined their connection, then share the actual relationship at the end.

The DNA testing website showed the amount of shared DNA between Cindy and Dorothy as 900 cM. Because the testing company can't quite know exactly how they are related, it defaults to a generalized 1st–2nd Cousin category. However, because Cindy is an adoptee, she can't tell me how she is actually related to Dorothy, and we cannot assume that she is Dorothy's first or second cousin. However, I can use her shared DNA amount with Dorothy, and their shared matches, as clues to work toward solving her mystery.

While the DNA testing websites do provide possible relationships, I prefer to use the "Shared cM Project" tool on the DNA Painter website. Using this tool is a super easy way to learn the different ways she might be related to Dorothy, someone with whom she's unfamiliar. When the amount of DNA shared between Cindy and Dorothy is entered into the entry field, these are the results, based on probability:

98%   Great-Grandparent, Great-Aunt/Uncle, Half Aunt/Uncle, 1C [First Cousin], Half Niece/Nephew, Great Niece/Nephew, Great-Grandchild

2%   Great-Great Aunt/Uncle, Great-Great Niece/Nephew, Half Great-Aunt/Uncle, Half Great-Niece/Nephew, Half 1C [Half First Cousin], 1C1R [Half First Cousin, Once Removed]

I choose to first focus on the 98 percent chance that Dorothy falls into one of the listed relationships for that percentage, but which one? Therein lies the necessity to do research, which can be complicated and time-consuming, but worth the effort in the end to get the answers we seek. In this scenario, Dorothy has a family tree, which is the best scenario, always, and her DNA results are attached to her in this family tree. When I look at the tree to which her DNA is attached, I see that she is now deceased, and was born in 1925. This tells me that she tested before her death, and that someone is managing her tree because she's been marked as deceased, which is what allows me to see her information. Her children are still living and therefore are hidden by the testing company for privacy reasons, so I can't see any information about them. Dorothy's parents Lucy and Alvin Sr. have several children, all of whom are deceased, and their names are listed. From here, I turn to my research plan. I want to rule out some relationships straight away, and to do that I have to make some initial hypotheses that might turn out to be incorrect, but that's okay. This will give me a starting point.

Because Dorothy was born in 1925 and Cindy was born in 1965, I hypothesize she is from a generation or two above Cindy, and therefore she is likely not going to be her first cousin, half niece, great niece, or great-grandchild. This leaves great-grandparent, great aunt, or half aunt. Since there are only forty years between Dorothy's birth and Cindy's, I think that makes her too young to be a great-grandparent. She could be a half-aunt, a sibling that shares one parent with one of Cindy's genetic parents, or she could be a full sibling of one of Cindy's genetic grandparents, making her a great aunt.

The next match to Cindy that also matches Dorothy is listed only by username MB88, and she and Cindy share 337 cM. I don't know how much MB88 shares with Dorothy because I can't see that. She does have a tree with very little information but that shows her own mother as Ellen, born in 1912. I then turn to DNA Painter again to see how Cindy could be related to MB88 and get the following:

48%	Great-Great-Aunt/Uncle, Half Great-Aunt/Uncle, Half 1C, 1C1R, Half Great-Niece/Nephew, Great-Great-Niece/Nephew
46%	Half GG-Niece/Nephew, Half GG-Aunt/Uncle, 2C Half 1C1R, 1C2R
5%	1C3R, Half 1C2R, Half 2C, 2C1R
<1%	Great-Aunt/Uncle, Great-Niece/Nephew

Because MB88's mother Ellen was born in 1912, I can make some more hypotheses to rule out relationships that probably don't fit. I go back to Dorothy's tree to see if I can find any information on Ellen there. The tree shows that Dorothy has a sister named Ellen who was born in 1912. If MB88 is the daughter of Ellen, and Ellen is the sister of Dorothy, that makes MB88 Dorothy's niece.

Because Cindy doesn't currently have any other close matches who share DNA with Dorothy, I can't yet determine exactly how they are related, but I make some assumptions again. I presume Cindy is not directly descended from Dorothy because they don't share enough DNA to be mother/daughter or grandmother/granddaughter, and I don't think Dorothy is old enough to be Cindy's great-grandmother. Because of this, I think Cindy's shared DNA with MB88 makes them likely to share a cousin relationship, and since Ellen is MB88's mother, and Cindy and MB88 don't share enough DNA to be mother/daughter or sisters, I know Cindy is not directly descended from Ellen. That leaves one of Dorothy's other siblings: Alvin Jr, Ivan, Harriet, or Melba as the potential ancestor. Without any more matches that are immediately apparent as fitting into Dorothy's tree, but knowing Cindy has an ancestor that is likely closely related to her, I concentrate on discovering more about her family members and their descendants.

Eventually, another match shows up who also matches Dorothy, and with whom Cindy shares 1054 cM, but there is no name, just the username DT93, and there is no tree. I also do not see this match in any other database to which I've submitted Cindy's raw DNA data or saliva for testing. At this point, then, my only option is to message the match to see if they're willing to offer information that will be helpful to Cindy's search and hope for a reply. Then it becomes a waiting game. Sometimes people answer quickly, but I've also had people respond to messages of inquiry anywhere from a few months to a few years later!

You can see how doing research for an adoptee or someone searching can quickly become complicated and frustrating. It took perseverance and many hours of work to piece enough information together to give Cindy her answer. Also, I had to start out with a few hypothetical scenarios, which isn't my favorite thing to do, but sometimes it's all I've got. Hypotheses worked out for me in this case, but they don't always, and I must backtrack. When DNA matches don't respond to inquiries, or refuse to answer, that can also slow down or stop research, as it did while I waited for DT93 to write back with helpful information. This can be very frustrating for people who are searching. Eventually I got a reply from DT93 that proved to be exactly what I needed to finalize an answer for Cindy.

If you're wondering how Dorothy is related to Cindy, she is Cindy's great-aunt, a sister to Cindy's genetic grandmother Melba. DT94 is Cindy's genetic half-nephew, son of her genetic half-brother Peter. Here's a tree that shows how all these people are related, with the DNA amount listed that is shared between Cindy and them (but not from them to each other).

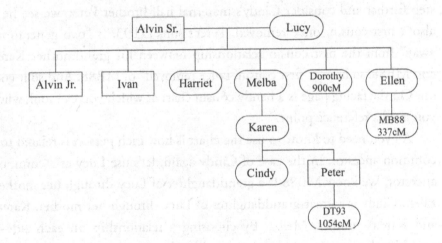

Confusing the Cousins: Removed Relationships

Since most companies sort DNA match results into cousin categories, the definition of "cousin" bears consideration. Who do you think of when you hear the word "cousin?" For most people, it's the children of their parents' siblings, which are called first cousins. However, there is more than one way to be a cousin! For example, how do you define the relationship between you and your mother's first cousin? Many people reason that their mother's first cousin must be their second cousin, and that is incorrect. Your mother's first cousin is your first cousin, once removed, which is abbreviated as 1C1R in the genealogy world. The second cousin for you in this scenario would be the child of your mother's first cousin.

Confused? You're not alone. I've seen a lot of people get confused by the "removed" relationships that go along with being a cousin. The "removed" relationship is the one that causes the most bewilderment in determining how two people who share autosomal DNA are related. It's a bit easier if you think of "removed" instead as "a generation away." Let's look again at the tree for Dorothy, Cindy, and MB88. Cindy is the genetic daughter of Karen, who is a first cousin of MB88 because their mothers, Melba and Ellen, are sisters. Cindy is "one generation away" from their first cousin relationship, therefore she is a "first cousin, once removed" of MB88. If we take that a step further and consider Cindy's maternal half-brother Peter, we see he is also a first cousin, once removed. Peter's son, DT93, is "two generations away" from the first cousin relationship between his grandmother Karen and MB88, so he is a "first cousin, twice removed" of MB88. And so it goes on. On the facing page is a handy cousin chart at which you can look when you need a reference point.

All you need to know to use the chart is how each person is related to a common ancestor. In the case of Cindy again, let's use Lucy as a common ancestor. We know MB88 is a granddaughter of Lucy through her mother, Ellen. Cindy is a great-granddaughter of Lucy through her mother, Karen, and Karen's mother, Melba. By choosing a relationship on each side—granddaughter on one side, great-granddaughter on the other—then meeting in the middle, we can again see that Cindy and MB88 are first cousins, once removed.

The big takeaways from this instructional are threefold: never assume anything in genealogy, do your research, and have fun! Regarding assumptions, unless you personally gave birth to them, you cannot know for sure how a

Your Grandparent

Common Ancestor	Grandparent	Great-Grandparent	2nd Great-Grandparent	3rd Great-Grandparent	4th Great-Grandparent	5th Great-Grandparent	6th Great-Grandparent	7th Great-Grandparent	8th Great-Grandparent	9th Great-Grandparent	10th Great-Grandparent
Grandparent	1st Cousin	1st Cousin, 1x Removed	1st Cousin, 2x Removed	1st Cousin, 3x Removed	1st Cousin, 4x Removed	1st Cousin, 5x Removed	1st Cousin, 6x Removed	1st Cousin, 7x Removed	1st Cousin, 8x Removed	1st Cousin, 9x Removed	1st Cousin, 10x Removed
Great-Grandparent	1st Cousin, 1x Removed	2nd Cousin	2nd Cousin, 1x Removed	2nd Cousin, 2x Removed	2nd Cousin, 3x Removed	2nd Cousin, 4x Removed	2nd Cousin, 5x Removed	2nd Cousin, 6x Removed	2nd Cousin, 7x Removed	2nd Cousin, 8x Removed	2nd Cousin, 9x Removed
2nd Great-Grandparent	1st Cousin, 2x Removed	2nd Cousin, 1x Removed	3rd Cousin	3rd Cousin, 1x Removed	3rd Cousin, 2x Removed	3rd Cousin, 3x Removed	3rd Cousin, 4x Removed	3rd Cousin, 5x Removed	3rd Cousin, 6x Removed	3rd Cousin, 7x Removed	3rd Cousin, 8x Removed
3rd Great-Grandparent	1st Cousin, 3x Removed	2nd Cousin, 2x Removed	3rd Cousin, 1x Removed	4th Cousin	4th Cousin, 1x Removed	4th Cousin, 2x Removed	4th Cousin, 3x Removed	4th Cousin, 4x Removed	4th Cousin, 5x Removed	4th Cousin, 6x Removed	4th Cousin, 7x Removed
4th Great-Grandparent	1st Cousin, 4x Removed	2nd Cousin, 3x Removed	3rd Cousin, 2x Removed	4th Cousin, 1x Removed	5th Cousin	5th Cousin, 1x Removed	5th Cousin, 2x Removed	5th Cousin, 3x Removed	5th Cousin, 4x Removed	5th Cousin, 5x Removed	5th Cousin, 6x Removed
5th Great-Grandparent	1st Cousin, 5x Removed	2nd Cousin, 4x Removed	3rd Cousin, 3x Removed	4th Cousin, 2x Removed	5th Cousin, 1x Removed	6th Cousin	6th Cousin, 1x Removed	6th Cousin, 2x Removed	6th Cousin, 3x Removed	6th Cousin, 4x Removed	6th Cousin, 5x Removed
6th Great-Grandparent	1st Cousin, 6x Removed	2nd Cousin, 5x Removed	3rd Cousin, 4x Removed	4th Cousin, 3x Removed	5th Cousin, 2x Removed	6th Cousin, 1x Removed	7th Cousin	7th Cousin, 1x Removed	7th Cousin, 2x Removed	7th Cousin, 3x Removed	7th Cousin, 4x Removed
7th Great-Grandparent	1st Cousin, 7x Removed	2nd Cousin, 6x Removed	3rd Cousin, 5x Removed	4th Cousin, 4x Removed	5th Cousin, 3x Removed	6th Cousin, 2x Removed	7th Cousin, 1x Removed	8th Cousin	8th Cousin, 1x Removed	8th Cousin, 2x Removed	8th Cousin, 3x Removed
8th Great-Grandparent	1st Cousin, 8x Removed	2nd Cousin, 7x Removed	3rd Cousin, 6x Removed	4th Cousin, 5x Removed	5th Cousin, 4x Removed	6th Cousin, 3x Removed	7th Cousin, 2x Removed	8th Cousin, 1x Removed	9th Cousin	9th Cousin, 1x Removed	9th Cousin, 2x Removed
9th Great-Grandparent	1st Cousin, 9x Removed	2nd Cousin, 8x Removed	3rd Cousin, 7x Removed	4th Cousin, 6x Removed	5th Cousin, 5x Removed	6th Cousin, 4x Removed	7th Cousin, 3x Removed	8th Cousin, 2x Removed	9th Cousin, 1x Removed	10th Cousin	10th Cousin, 1x Removed
10th Great-Grandparent	1st Cousin, 10x Removed	2nd Cousin, 9x Removed	3rd Cousin, 8x Removed	4th Cousin, 7x Removed	5th Cousin, 6x Removed	6th Cousin, 5x Removed	7th Cousin, 4x Removed	8th Cousin, 3x Removed	9th Cousin, 2x Removed	10th Cousin, 1x Removed	11th Cousin

Their Grandparent

Cousin Calculator

match is related to you based on the designation given by the testing company. A lot of people make assumptions about relationships based on their personal feelings, or a generalized relationship description. While it's hard to push that aside, you must learn to be methodical with every single match. Surprises happen in DNA testing and that can be unsettling. Your feelings, whether negative or positive, will not change the facts.

As to research, if you want to determine the relationship of a DNA match, you must build your tree with direct ancestors, branch it sideways and down, and place them in the proper position within your tree. Then, confirm it. Otherwise, you're guessing, and that can be disruptive and unethical, especially if you make an incorrect assumption that causes a family rift. Lastly, while genealogy can be complicated and messy, it can also be fun. I love the process of making connections, solving mysteries both big and small, and discovering and discussing shared ancestry with newfound cousins. Utilize hypotheses temporarily but don't make them into permanent assumptions, do your research, and enjoy the genetic genealogy adventure!

Your Ancestral Cloak of Autosomal DNA

Because autosomal DNA comes to us in so many pieces, it has always reminded me of a beautiful patchwork cloak that is manifested by the physical essence of the ancestors from whom we inherited our autosomal DNA. I feel mine wrapped around me, reminding me frequently of who I am and where I come from. Through virtue of our inheritance of their DNA, we each are a unique embodied manifestation of the ancestors' physical makeup and lived stories. Whether we know anything about our genealogical ancestors or not, we each carry a one-of-a-kind cloak with us that is comprised of genetic pieces from many of them.

The ancestral cloak is a patchwork of energy that represents the genetic signatures of the people from whom we've inherited our DNA, and the culture and heritage from which their own ancestors hailed. It does not represent the current, real-time energy of living genealogical family, so there are no living dysfunctional patterns within it. The cloak takes the best bits of our genetic ancestry, the beautiful and positive parts of it, and envelops us in a bubble of love and protection.

For a few of us, the cloak is mostly one color, a tone-on-tone variation of shades that represent the varieties of many peoples from one place. For example, a friend of mine is Irish, her parents are Irish immigrants, her ethnicity estimate shows her as 98 percent Irish. Her cloak is imagined by her to be in many shades of shimmering green, much like the land of her ancestors, with tiny flecks of other colors to represent those who hailed from elsewhere.

My own ethnicity estimate, and my genealogy research, shows a genetic heritage that is a lot more diverse. My ancestors hailed from many places, they were traveling folk who crossed continents and oceans in search of something better. I envision my ancestral cloak to be multi-colored, in warm tones reminiscent of the elements, resistant to the wild weather sometimes encountered by those who travel long distances.

For some, due to circumstances that keep them from the knowledge of their genetic ancestors, it can be hard to see, or feel, their ancestral cloak. This doesn't mean it does not exist! The cloak is there and creating a mental image of it simply requires a peek behind the curtain of DNA. This can be accomplished with DNA testing. Even those who don't want to find out more about the particular people to whom they are related genetically can test to get a glimpse of their roots. Ethnicity is always an estimate, but it can still give the information needed to envision a cloak. Perhaps the information obtained from a DNA test can one day be used to further knowledge by working with DNA matches to engage in the research needed to provide yourself with answers about your roots.

Journal Magic: Your Autosomal Cloak

You will need your journal and pen, markers or pencils in a variety of colors, and a seven-day candle. Clear the energy of your space with your clearing spray and state the intention that you are creating a love-filled, creative, and self-assured atmosphere. Light your seven-day candle. Open the session in your usual way.

Stare into your candle flame for a few minutes and think over your family story. Think about your ancestors. Where did they come from? What cultures do they represent to you? If you have DNA results, look at your ethnicity estimate. Does it fully represent what you know about your ancestry? Or does it have some elements that don't quite make sense? How might you represent in your cloak the ancestors for whom you will likely not ever know anything? You can refer to any trees you've created if that helps you create a mental picture of your ancestors and their roots.

Think now on what an ancestral cloak might look like for you. This is a creative process and nothing is too outlandish. Some people prefer simple, functional clothing. Others (like Leo me!) prefer clothing that is a bit more outspoken in its appearance. The ancestral cloak is a mind's eye manifestation of the positive genetic energies that surround you, that you can mentally pull close to you and wrap around you whenever you desire. Your cloak is for you alone, no one else's in the world will be like yours, so envision it as you will.

Write down a description of your ancestral cloak. What does it look like? What does it feel like? Are there many colors, or just one? Is it long and flowing, or short and snug to the skin? Is there a hood? Pockets? If you are comfortable doing so, draw a picture of your cloak. It doesn't have to be a perfect drawing; it only needs to serve as a point of reference for times you might want to refer to your original thoughts about how it looked and felt to you. Remember, this cloak is only constructed of positive energies, so do not allow the dynamics of negativity that might be present in your life to be part of its construction. For example, I have a known recent ancestor about whom I do not feel very positive much of the time, and my healing around this person is a work in progress. The only positive thing I can usually think about them is that their hair color is very pretty. So, their contribution to my cloak's energetic construction is the energy of beauty. That's it, nothing else. Perhaps one day it will be more, but for now, that one thing is just fine!

When you are finished writing, drawing, or both, create an image in your mind of yourself in this ancestral cloak. Feel its gentle weight on your shoulders, allow it to wrap you in a bubble of love and protection from the people whose physical essence you carry within you.

Snuff your candle, close your journal session, and clear your space with the clearing spray.

The Ragged Edges

The ancestral cloak can look or feel a bit ragged in places where negative ancestral energies sneak into its weaving. This must not be allowed, so attend to it frequently. I consider my own cloak to always be a work in progress, with mending needed here and there, to keep it looking and feeling its best. Much as some people might check their protective shields for breaks and then repair them energetically, so too do I assess my ancestral cloak for frayed edges and worn cuffs, so to speak. My cloak is a manifestation of only the positive attributes and qualities of my ancestors, but I must work to keep it that way. My ongoing process of ancestral healing is tied to the integrity of my cloak, which is why I am always looking to engage with the process of working through negative ancestral patterns. Either way, I do not allow negativity to energetically sit on my shoulders. Since I wear my ancestral cloak as a sacred energetic object in which only positive energies are allowed to reside, I must work to ensure it stays that way.

Remember, your ancestral cloak is an energetic manifestation of the positive aspects of the ancestors whose DNA you carry within you. Use your mind's eye image of your cloak as a reminder of who you are, where you come from, and let it help you to stand tall within your own sovereignty as you purposely and intentionally live life in your own beautiful way.

8

Mitochondrial DNA: The Crown

Your body is as ancient as the clay of the universe from which it is made; and your feet on the ground are a constant connection with the earth. Your feet bring your private clay in touch with the ancient, mother clay from which you first emerged.

—John O'Donohue

Mitochondrial DNA refers to the DNA found inside mitochondria, which are a type of organelle found in almost all complex cells. They are known as the power plants of the cell because they supply an enzyme or, more accurately, a co-enzyme, known as adenosine triphosphate (ATP). This ATP is the source for the chemical energy needed by a cell to perform a wide range of functions. Mitochondria once functioned independently from the host cell but around two billion years ago, they formed a symbiotic relationship and the mitochondria moved into the host cell's structure. The mitochondria provide energy for the host cell, and the host cell provides shelter for the mitochondria.

Mitochondria have their own distinct and separate DNA. It's tightly coiled and when unwrapped, it is a circular double helix structure. Mitochondrial DNA (mtDNA) is present in both males and females. However, it is inherited strictly on the maternal line and therefore only females, or XX people, can pass it to their children. A female's children will have her mtDNA.

A male's children will not have his mtDNA but rather will have the mtDNA of the female/XX person who provides the egg for their conception, and who then carries them and births them. (In the case of surrogate pregnancies, there is no transfer of DNA in gestational surrogacy. Also, as noted in chapter 3— The Language of Genealogy, three parent individuals conceived by mitochondrial transfer fall outside the scope of this book.) The female's mitochondria are contained in large amounts inside the egg waiting to be fertilized. The male's mitochondria contribute to the creation of an embryo by creating the energy needed to power the sperms' tails as they swim to fertilize the egg, but this genetic propeller does not enter the egg upon fertilization.[10]

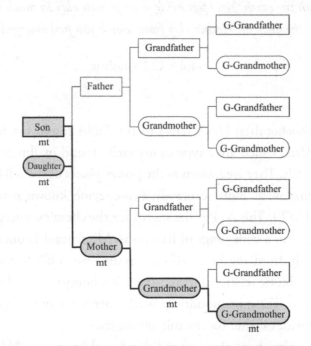

Mitochondrial DNA is passed down exclusively from the mother/maternal/XX line to both XX and XY genetic offspring. The direct line of mitochondrial DNA inheritance is known as the mother line or the maternal line.

[10] There is a case study from 2004 that suggests a mixed mitochondrial inheritance, both maternal and paternal, due to a labeling mutation in autosomal DNA. This possibility is debated within the scientific community and discussion of it falls outside the scope of this book.

There is a staggering amount of magic and power in our mitochondria. Its independent DNA structure has been a fascination to me since I discovered its ability to manifest energy for the cell. The microscopic circular bit of genetic substance that lives inside the mitochondria of every one of our complex cells connects us along our maternal line to a lineage of women that is thousands and thousands of years old. Stop and think about the enormity of this for one moment. Your mitochondria, passed to you by the woman/XX person from whose egg you were conceived, is an exact replica of the same mitochondria that has been passed along for countless generations.

The Mitochondrial Mothers and the Molecular Clock

The mitochondrial mothers are ancient women who represent moments in time. From the singular ancient mother whose mitochondria serves as the source for all humans alive today, to the multiple ancient mothers whose genetic mutations marked a genetic shift for her descendants, we each touch the energy of their existence simply by being ourselves. The bloodlines of ancient mothers evolved into distinct groups over the millennia with small genetic mutations that are classed into haplogroups. These form their own sort of tree, much like a family tree.

Because mitochondria have their own DNA, separate from the main cell's DNA that resides in the cell's nucleus, this makes it an excellent resource for molecular and evolutionary biologists. Why? Mitochondrial DNA doesn't experience evolutionary pressure to recombine on a regular basis like autosomal DNA, which undergoes a shuffle with every generation. Mitochondrial DNA is passed from female/XX person to offspring unchanged, save for mutations (tiny, usually harmless, changes) that occur at a very slow, predictable rate. Because of this exceedingly slow rate of change, mitochondrial DNA provides the necessities for what is known as a "molecular clock." The idea behind this clock is that random mutations add up at a relatively constant rate over time. Since scientists have determined the average mutation rate (how often these mutations occur)

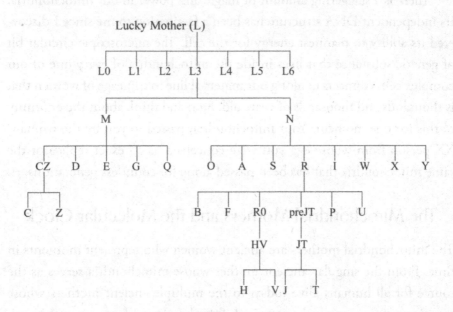

The current phylogenetic tree for mitochondrial DNA (PhyloTree mt Build 17, Feb 2016). The letters represent the major haplogroups, and super haplogroups N, M, and R. The tree shows how they all descend from haplogroup L, which belonged to the common ancestral mother for all humans alive today. Because the science, and scientists' knowledge, continues to evolve, the structure of this tree will likely change with the next build update.

of mitochondrial DNA, they are able to extrapolate how long ago two people shared a common ancestor. This can't be reliably done with autosomal DNA because, unlike mitochondrial DNA, it experiences evolutionary pressure to change and it recombines with every generation, therefore making it harder to track through time.

So, what exactly does this all mean? I'll use myself as an example.

I have done a mitochondrial DNA test with Family Tree DNA, and I have been determined to fall into the mitochondrial haplogroup of H1. This H1 mtDNA was passed down to me from my mother, and she got it from her mother, and so on, back to the woman who was the first H1. How was she the first? In the simplest explanation, her mother was H, and when this H1 daughter was conceived, a mutation occurred in her mitochondrial DNA that caused a slight shift, and thus resulted in her being the first H1 daughter and, eventually, mother. Scientists studying mitochondrial DNA use their molecular clock technique to determine these shifts, and so the phylogenetic tree for mitochondrial DNA continues to be developed. My H1 (and everyone who is H1) is placed in the haplotree for the top-level H haplogroup, which is part of the mitochondrial DNA phylogenetic tree that shows all the top-level haplogroups.

This progression is able to be determined because scientists have used the molecular clock to trace human female migration and can pinpoint the ancestors of a haplogroup mother, much as we can use a family tree to trace our own ancestors.

In another example, my husband's mitochondrial haplogroup is H1c1b. He also falls under the top-level H haplogroup and is placed in the H haplotree, but his branch is a placed a bit further down than mine. This means that we both share an H1 ancestor, but his female line has since had mutations that reclass them into H1c1b, whereas I am still H1. We also both descend from the first woman who had an H haplogroup and all its predecessors, which eventually lead back to L.

There are ancient continental populations associated with clusters of mitochondrial haplogroups. The origin of all of them lies in Africa with Lucky Mother and her L haplogroup. New haplogroups arose over many thousands of years as people slowly migrated across the earth.

Lucky Mother

Mitochondrial DNA's lineage can be a bit amorphous and complicated, but the simple explanation is that all humans alive today are descended from one woman. I refer to her as "Lucky Mother" because that was the preferred name by the scientists who discovered her. Back in 1987, three scientists,

Rebecca Cann, Mark Stoneking, and Allan Wilson, discovered that all humans alive today are descended from one woman. When people hear this, it's common to hear the response, "How could there have only been one woman alive?" Well, there wasn't only one woman alive at the time. This ancient mother was part of a population that had different mtDNA types, but those other types eventually went extinct because the descendants of those other females either didn't have offspring or had only male offspring. Her particular mitochondrial DNA survived and mutated into the many different types currently found in the world today. She certainly had no idea that she would be the ancestress of a mitochondrial DNA line that would propagate and survive over thousands and thousands of years. When the news came out of Lucky Mother's discovery, she was dubbed Mitochondrial Eve (mtEve) by the mainstream media, which only adds to the confusion as she is now often conflated with the biblical Eve. They are not the same. Mark Stoneking shared,

> *This random extinction of lineages, coupled with a single origin of DNA, is sufficient to guarantee that all of the variation in all of our genes has to trace back to a single common ancestor at some point in the past. And even though all of our genes have ancestors, our mtDNA ancestor was not the ancestor of all of our other genes—they trace their ancestry back to different individuals (and even different species), living at different times in different places.*
>
> *This is why the "mtEve" designation is incorrect—Allan Wilson favored the term "lucky mother," to emphasize the role of chance in the survival of mtDNA lineages over time, but I guess it just wasn't as catchy a term as Mitochondrial Eve.[11]*

---

[11] Gizmodo; "The scientists behind Mitochondrial Eve tell us about the 'lucky mother' who changed human evolution forever"—by Alasdair Wilkins: *https://gizmodo.com*

In other words, she cannot be the biblical Eve, because our different types of DNA—mitochondrial, Y, X, and autosomal—all have different sources. Lucky Mother is the original source of our mitochondrial DNA.

Your Crown of Mitochondrial DNA

I first experienced the magic of my mother line when my daughter was giving birth to her first son. Due to a challenging medical condition that would affect her ability to push during delivery, another medical condition that greatly increased the chance of fetal demise after thirty-seven weeks' gestation, along with my grandson being in a breech (feet first) presentation, she was scheduled for a cesarean section three weeks before her due date. That wasn't ideal, as those last weeks are critical to the final development of the fetus's lungs, but it was necessary. The day came and off we went to the hospital.

In addition to my daughter's partner, I was allowed to be in the operating room (OR) because I worked at the same hospital in the surgical intensive care unit and knew the OR staff, so I was able to pull some strings. The rest of our family was in the waiting room. I sat at my daughter's shoulder, her partner was at the other, all of us behind a surgical drape to obscure the details of the surgery in progress, as the sight of that can be quite disconcerting to many people. The first inkling that something was amiss was when the obstetrician requested the circulating nurse to call her partner to assist with the delivery. As a registered nurse who'd previously worked in labor and delivery, I recognized the urgency in her tone. I was able to peer over the drape and noticed a large amount of blood-saturated lap sponges (small sterile cloths used during surgery to absorb blood) in multiple pans. My daughter was hemorrhaging.

The second obstetrician arrived, and my grandson was delivered quickly, held up over the drape for us to see, then handed over to the newborn nursery staff. We waited for the usual post-delivery cry which was not immediately forthcoming. This time I stood up to look over the drape, glanced briefly at the two obstetricians whose hands were flying to cauterize bleeding vessels and suture my daughter's incision closed, then looked across the room to see that my grandson was blue and non-responsive, and the nursery staff were resuscitating him. I sat back down and saw my daughter's beautiful gray eyes looking up at me and her asking, "Is everything okay?" I smiled and nodded to her to indicate that yes, all was fine, and I began to silently pray.

I then looked at my watch—over a minute since his delivery and still no cry—and I mentally continued to mumble my prayer for strength to handle what might be coming. My daughter and her partner kept looking at me with big eyes, their fear apparent. As I stroked my daughter's hair, I felt a pulling sensation in the middle of my back. I turned around to see what was there but saw nothing. Suddenly, I felt like I'd gotten an infusion of pure fire energy and I somehow knew the women of my mother line—my mother's mother, her mother, and her mother, and beyond—had arrived. My grandmother's presence was much stronger, but I could feel many women in the room. I sensed the links in our maternal chain that connected us, womb to womb to womb, stretched back through time. They were there in that operating room with us as the newest link in our chain, my daughter, birthed her own child, as each one of them had done in the years, centuries, and millennia before us. Whatever happened, good or bad, they were there with us. I closed my eyes, drew in a deep breath of their powerful energy, and placed my hand on my daughter's shoulder while I quietly exhaled, to share it with her. At that moment, my grandson began to cry, then we all began to cry. My daughter was a mother, and I was a grandmother.

Soon after, my grandson's bassinet was wheeled out to the nursery and his father followed. The nurse anesthetist managing my daughter's epidural waggled her eyebrows at me, I nodded yes, and my daughter was sent off to lightly sleep with the help of a sedative medication while her surgery was completed. Before I left the room, I peered over the drape again and I was shaken by the bowls of lap sponges that were saturated with my daughter's birthing blood. I was not a nurse in that moment, but a mother, and I was scared for my daughter. I caught the glimpse of her obstetrician who told me, "She's good. Really." I chose to trust, kissed my daughter's forehead, and went out to the waiting room to share the blessed news that our family's newest member had arrived and both mother and son were well. (My daughter was very weak after delivery from the blood loss but recovered without incident, and my grandson is now a healthy and busy young teenager.)

The magic of that moment, of being energetically surrounded by my mother line as my own daughter gave birth, changed me at a cellular level. I felt revitalized, like my mind had opened up to an unknown part of myself that had always been there. It was spectacular, and I was fascinated by the concept of this miraculous, near-endless chain of mothers. I'd worked for years with my female ancestors almost exclusively, but they were pulled from across my tree on both maternal and paternal sides. Of course I always knew at some level that I had a direct female line, but I'd never really considered the magnitude of it, or the deep magic that it held.

In 2013, when I reorganized my approach to genealogy and began to intentionally incorporate magic into my work, I also began to do more research about mitochondrial DNA. Its independent nature was fascinating to me. Looking back on my early years, I realized that, in my family, there was always a big to-do whenever one of the men had a son, but there was never anything celebratory about a woman having a daughter (other than the usual baby congrats), so it hadn't ever really occurred to me that my own mother line was also quite significant.

It also occurred to me, after I learned more about the physical structure and shape of our mitochondria, that it resembles a crown. It seemed to me to be a rather pompous symbol to attribute to myself and my mitochondrial DNA, but when I started thinking about what the crown symbolizes—royalty, power, legitimacy, wealth, victory, divinity, glory—three words really stuck with me:

- Divinity: The magic of the maternal line carries the divine alchemy of the sacred feminine into our physical being.

- Legitimacy: Our mitochondrial DNA legitimizes our existence and our innate right to be here exactly as we were made.

- Power: Mitochondria literally powers bodily function.

My mitochondrial crown is divine, legitimate, and powerful. It stands as a fiery symbol of the women through time who've birthed the daughters who have then passed this essential DNA to their own children. Every function of my body, both voluntary and involuntary, is powered by the mitochondria in each cell. Every breath I take is a direct result of my recent and ancient mother line, women who grew children in their bellies who grew to birth their own. The crown also symbolizes my royalty—I am the queen of my personal realm—and its wealth, my body and its physical and mental being. The victory symbolized by my crown is a result of my battles to be heard, to be seen, my struggle to be healthy and move my body in spite of its limitations, my journey through life as I strive to live it to its fullest extent. We all have defeats, of course, but the victory lies in the efforts we make to be our best selves.

Journal Magic: Your Mitochondrial Crown

You will need your journal and pen, markers or pencils in a variety of colors, and your orange seven-day candle. Clear the energy of your space with your clearing spray and state the intention that you are creating a love-filled and creative atmosphere. Light your candle. Open the session in your usual way.

Stare into your candle flame for a few minutes and think about your mother line. Where did they come from? What cultures do they represent to you? If you have autosomal DNA results (like Ancestry), look at your ethnicity estimate. Can you attribute certain bits of it to your mother line's ancestry? If you've got a mitochondrial haplogroup designation from 23andMe or Family Tree DNA, look at its placement on the phylogenetic tree for mitochondrial DNA. How many major haplogroup mutations have happened in your mother line that lead you back to Lucky Mother?

Do some research online about your mitochondrial haplogroup. Where did it originate? Think about the places the ancient mothers lived during the many lifetimes before yours. How might you represent in your crown these ancient mothers? Your mother? You and your own divinity, legitimacy, and power? You can refer to any trees you've created if that helps you create a mental picture of your mother line and its roots. If you feel you need to leave out the mothers known to you in this lifetime and skip to the mothers of the past, do so.

Think now on your crown's appearance. As with the cloak, this is a creative process. Your crown is an energetic symbol of your own divine being, the legitimacy of your existence, and the power you carry within that fires your mind and body and propels both along your life path. Write down a description of your crown. What does it look like? What does it feel like? Is it heavy or light? What's it made of? Flowers? Precious metals? Are there many colors, or just one? Is it simple or ornate? If you are comfortable doing so, draw a picture of your crown. It doesn't have to be a perfect drawing; it only needs to serve as a point of reference for the times you might want to refer to your original thoughts about how it looked and felt to you. Remember, like the cloak, your crown is constructed of only positive energies, so do not allow the dynamics of negativity that might be present in your life to be part of its construction.

When you are finished writing, drawing, or both, create an image in your mind of yourself wearing your crown. Feel its weight on your head, feel it fueling your energy with its ancient mother power.

Snuff your candle, close your journal session, and clear your space with the clearing spray.

Chips and Cracks

Much like the ancestral cloak's energy can feel ragged, the crown can look or feel chipped or cracked in places where negative ancestral energies sneak into its weaving. Again, this must not be allowed, so attend to it frequently.

My energetic crown will occasionally need mending, and I do this with an ongoing process of ancestral healing that is tied to the integrity of my crown. I do not allow negativity to energetically sit on my head. My crown is a sacred representation of my mother line energies and I work to keep it clear and clean.

Your crown is a positive energetic manifestation of the mitochondrial mothers' power. Use the mental image of your crown as a reminder that you are divine, your life and your personal expression is legitimate, and you carry the energy of a sovereign within your being, fueled by the ancient mothers.

Honoring the Mother Line

Consider this short ritual to pay homage to those in your direct mother line. Perhaps you know many names, none, or just a few. Eventually we all get to the point where we don't know the name of the next ancestral woman in our line. Whether you know none, one, several, or many, take the time to envision and honor the mothers of old.

Materials Needed:
   Red chime/spell or taper candle
   Petals from a red flower, like a rose or carnation
   A piece of moonstone
   A small cloth bag
   Journal and pen

Instructions:
Cleanse the energy of your space with your clearing spray. Sprinkle the red flower petals around the base of your candle. As you do so, close your eyes, quiet your mind, and envision your mother line. Names and faces are not necessary, the mother line exists within each of us whether or not we can visualize them. If you feel any negativity in the moment, any trials or tribulations, try to lay them aside and simply picture the blood moving within you, through you, the ancient and wise mitochondria powering each breath, each movement.

Open your eyes and light your candle. If there are names from your direct maternal line that you'd specifically like to honor, say them now. If you don't know any names, that's okay. If you'd prefer not to say anything at all and just quietly honor the divinity within yourself, do that. I will use myself and my mother line as the example, and please substitute your own mother line names if you know them and plan to speak them aloud:

I light this candle in honor of my known mother line ancestors: Susan, Mabel, Louisa, Mathilde, Celeste, Eurasie, Nanette, Françoise, Anna Maria, and Anna Maria, and in honor of those unknown to me by name, all of whose energy I carry within me.

OR

I light this candle in honor of my mother line ancestors, whose energy I carry within me.

As your candle burns, sit quietly and think on your connection to your mother line. If you've been to the location of the known source of your mother line, revel in the memory. If not, imagine yourself there, walking in the same footsteps as these women who walked the earth before you. If you prefer, sink into the watery memories of the womb and the sacred feminine. Hear the heartbeats and the swoosh of blood that flowed through you as you were beautifully built, cell by cell. Breathe in and breathe out, feel the power of 150,000-plus years move through you from root to crown. You are a glorious child, and a manifestation of ancient mother knowing, a genetic melody, a song of blood and water and fire and earth and sky, uniquely positioned in this world to manifest a destiny of your choosing.

When you are done, let the candles burn down. Gather the flower petals and place them into the small bag. Place them under your pillow and go to bed with the intent that you will dream of the ancient mothers. Be sure to place your journal and pen at your bedside. When you wake up, immediately write down anything you remember about your dream time.

The End of the Line

We all know people who carry and birth children and we know people who do not, for various reasons. The people who don't have genetic offspring are no less alive than the people who do, however, remaining childless is the one definite way not to pass down any DNA at all, including mitochondrial DNA. All people alive today are descendants of Lucky Mother, however, for the females/XX people who do not birth female offspring of their own to pass along their mitochondrial DNA, their personal branch of their mito-chondrial line ends. That doesn't mean the haplogroup ends though, only the line on which there are no further female offspring. Just as various mito-chondrial lines from Lucky Mother's time slowly went extinct until hers was the only one left that has living descendants, so too do they continue to do so today.

Sonning Out, and the Final mtDNA Daughter

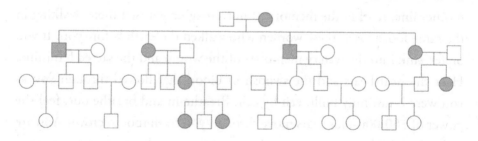

Mary, and her descendants who inherited her mitochondrial DNA, are in gray. Notice that not all of her great-grandchildren have her mtDNA because there were only sons born in a line and thus have "sonned out," or, the daughter of a line did not have children, and so is the final mtDNA daughter of that line.

I will give myself as an additional example of a mother/maternal line that is likely ended. I gave birth to two daughters who carry an exact replica of my H1 haplogroup in their mitochondrial DNA. However, my oldest daughter has chosen not to have children. My youngest daughter has two sons who, while they do also carry my H1 mitochondrial DNA, are males and cannot pass it along to their children. Unless one of my daughters gives birth to a daughter who will then birth a daughter, and so on, my line of H1 has ended. Perhaps my granddaughter might've had a mutation in her H1 that caused a slight adjustment to the DNA, thus starting a new branch. Alas, without further female descendants, this won't happen on my direct line. My sister is also H1, she has three daughters and perhaps one of them will birth a daughter to carry on our H1 line. If that happens, it's as close as I will get to a continuation of my direct mother line, through my sister, because we share the same mother and the same direct maternal line. If her daughters do not have a daughter among them, the next closest female descendant of my maternal line is through my mother's cousin who has a daughter and granddaughters. Here's a chart to make things a bit clearer.

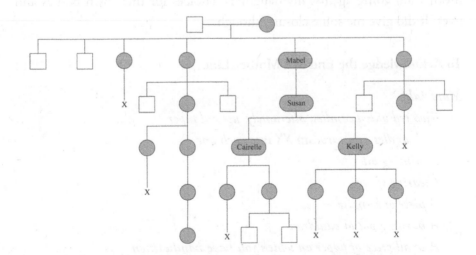

Of course, there are thousands and thousands of other H1 mitochondrial lines in the world. The ending of my line is not a huge loss to the overall continuation of the H1 line. However, you can see how these random endings could eventually wipe a line out of existence. Of course, I also have my own personal feelings about the ending of my direct female line. While I do have two daughters, and I feel connected to these mothers of my line, the women who, back through time, gave birth to a daughter who would give birth to the next daughter, all the way down to me, I will likely not have a further continuation of my personal mitochondrial DNA line. I find it makes me a bit sad that there will not one day be a direct line granddaughter who looks back to me, much as I look back to my own Anna Maria, who crossed an ocean for a chance at a better life and gave birth on a ship en route! She died a mere three years after her arrival to the harsh conditions of early Louisiana, but I feel her nonetheless as a strong energetic presence in my life, she is a beautiful jewel in my crown, and a reminder of the strength and perseverance of the women who came before me.

It occurred to me that I should acknowledge my feelings of sadness with a short ritual to mark the ending of my mother line. Of course, that doesn't change anything, nor do I wish to push a change because to do so would mean I am going against my daughters' choices for their own bodies and lives. It did give me some closure, though.

To Acknowledge the End of a Mother Line

Materials:
   Two red vulva candles; alternately, use red taper
      candles and carve an XX into each one
   Anointing oil
   Clearing spray
   A piece of kunzite
   A burning pot or cauldron
   A small piece of paper on which you have handwritten
      the names of your direct mother line ancestors; if you
      don't know, write "my direct mother line"

Instructions:

Cleanse your space with your clearing spray. Anoint your candles from top to bottom, three times each, and envision the women in your direct mother line who came before you. Place the kunzite in the middle of the two candles. Light the first candle and say:

> *I honor you, recent and ancient mothers of my particular line, those known to me by name and those whose names are lost to the mists of time. I honor the essence of your physical being that lives within me and powers my being. I honor the sacrifices made that ensured its survival from you to me. I acknowledge and honor the burden and joy of your childbearing. I honor your life, however brief or long it may have been.*

Light the second candle and say:

> *I am (or my daughter is) the last daughter of this particular mother line. I stand here as a proud representative of all who have come before me. Bless me as I walk my path and do the work that will contribute to the continuance of other sacred mother lines. Thank you for your essence that powers my being.*

Light the name paper and let it burn in the cauldron. Let both candles burn down. Keep the kunzite next to a framed photo of a female ancestor in your direct line, or a photo of yourself. Take time to sit with it occasionally to remind you that your time here on earth is powerful in many ways, and that you contribute to the legacy of women everywhere with the work you do.

 Add kunzite to your genealogy toolbox to have on hand when you need to find peace within your heart regarding any type of ending.

9

X-DNA: The Chalice

Know that when my life is through, like a river
flowing to the sea, I will flow right into you.

—Patti Tuck, Love Flows Like a River

X-DNA is the DNA that seems to be most confusing to people, mainly because of its inheritance pattern. X-DNA and Y-DNA are both sex chromosomes that, in one of two configurations, make us genetically male or female. Because of that, it is sometimes presumed that X-DNA is associated only with females because Y-DNA is associated only with males in that they can receive it only from their father/XY parent and pass it along to only their male children. However, X-DNA is carried by everyone and is passed down along an intricate and beautiful pathway from various ancestors in a precise order. It flows down from the ancestors into our physical being, carrying along with it the ingredients we can use to manifest a magical life.

Like pretty much everything else in DNA genealogy, X-DNA also can be placed into a tree form that shows the potential ancestors from whom we can carry X-DNA. Like autosomal DNA, the chance of carrying X-DNA from these potential ancestors decreases with each generation removed from them. The inheritance pattern of X-DNA is also different for females and males, unlike with autosomal DNA, which is inherited in a similar way. It seems complicated at first but when made visual in tree form becomes a bit clearer. As a sex chromosome, X-DNA's presence or absence from our father/XY parent is what determines us genetically as either female/XX or male/XY. Remember, males get Y-DNA from their father, females get X-DNA from their father. Mothers pass along X-DNA to all of their children. It's a bit more tangled than that, however, we can use that simple math problem that we used with autosomal DNA to serve again as an easy way to think about it:

50 + 50 = 100

We always get fifty of X from the egg of our mother/XX parent. Whether or not we get another fifty of X from our father/XY parent depends on whether the fertilizing sperm carries X or Y to the egg during fertilization. Consider these two scenarios which will result in either female/XX or male/XY offspring:

50 of mom's (XX parent's) X + 50 of dad's (XY parent's) X = 100, or XX

50 of mom's (XX parent's) X + 50 of dad's (XY parent's) Y = 100, or XY

Only female offspring will receive X-DNA from the father/XY parent, making them an XX person. Males receive a Y from him instead of an X, making them an XY person. The easiest way to think about X-DNA inheritance is to consider the lottery analogy again. We each need one hundred ping-pong balls in total to create our XX or XY. We get fifty from each parent. Our mother, or XX parent, has one hundred individual ping-pong balls to give us but we can take only fifty from her. Females are the movers and shakers of X-DNA, so what we get from her is completely randomized, much like a lottery drawing, and similar to how our autosomal DNA is passed down from both parents. Our father, or XY parent, also has one hundred individual ping-pong balls to give. However, there is no randomization in how his X and Y are passed to his offspring. His one-hundred ping-pong balls are split into two sets with fifty ping-pong balls in each, one set labeled X, the other set labeled Y, that cannot be broken apart. Each person receives either a set of fifty X ping-pong balls or a set of fifty Y ping-pong balls. The X set, once passed along in an exact copy to every female/XX child, can then be broken apart by her to randomly pass along to her own children, both female and male. The Y set, however, remains intact when passed to a male/XY child, who will then pass it along intact to every male child of his.

Because males and females don't inherit X-DNA in the same way, let's take a look at the inheritance patterns of each.

The tree on page 116 shows how females access X-DNA through their mother and father. The inheritance of X-DNA through the father/XY line, in addition to autosomal DNA, is another way women are able to access the divine masculine of their father's father line, and other male ancestors.

The tree on page 117 shows how males can access X-DNA only through their mother/XX parent. The other half of their sex chromosome is from the Y-DNA they inherited in an exact copy through their father/XY line. The inheritance of X-DNA from their mother is another way, in addition to autosomal and mitochondrial DNA, in which men access the sacred feminine.

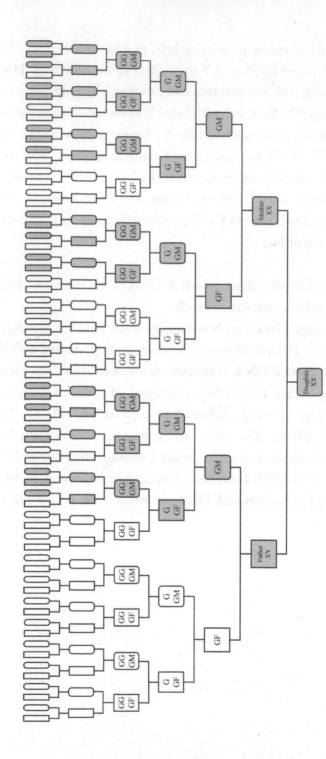

Female/XX Inheritance of X-DNA

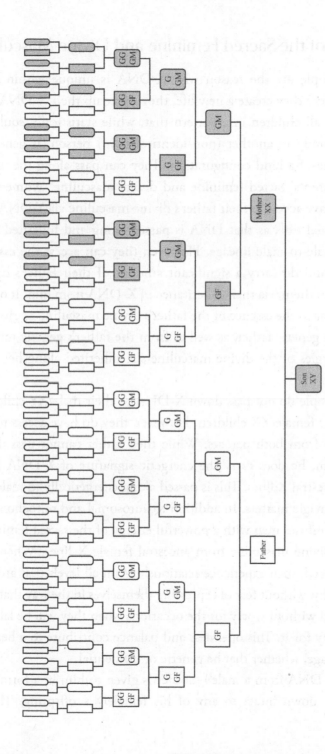

Male/XY Inheritance of X-DNA

Inheritance of the Sacred Feminine and Divine Masculine

Women/XX people are the reason why X-DNA is unique within each person. Every time they create a new life, they shake up their X-DNA and pass it along to all children in a pattern that, while statistically could be replicated randomly in another (non-identical twin) person, is generally considered a one-of-a-kind configuration. They can pass along the magic of their own parents' sacred feminine and divine masculine. Women/XX people do not have access to their father's divine masculine via Y-DNA and the direct paternal line, as that DNA is passed along and inherited only on a male-to-male-to-male lineage. However, they can access the essence of that energy and do carry a significant amount of their father's divine masculine within them, via their inheritance of X-DNA from him. It opens an energetic door to the essence of the father's divine masculine as given to him by his own genetic father, as well as from the father's genetic mother and all the energies of the divine masculine she inherited along her own ancestral X lines.

Men/XY people do not pass down X-DNA to their male/XY children, but only to their female/XX children. However, they do have access to the sacred feminine from both parents. While their father cannot pass down X-DNA to them, he does carry the energetic signature of X-DNA from his mother's ancestral X lines. This is passed along energetically to male/XY offspring. This magic matters. In addition to autosomal and mitochondrial DNA, X-DNA infuses men with a powerful energy of the sacred feminine, as well as the divine masculine from ancestral female X lines. When this energy is embraced, men experience relationships on all levels that are balanced and healthy, without fear of expressing themselves in the way that best serves them, and without worry for the occasions when they will be labeled in a negative way for it. This openness and balance contribute to a healthy descendant lineage, whether that be genetic or influential.

Also, the X-DNA from a male's mother is given to him in a form that must be passed down intact to any of his female/XX offspring. This is powerful. Stop and think about that for a moment. Granddaughters have an exact copy of the X-DNA given to their father by their paternal grand-mother. In an example, my father has three daughters: me, and my two sisters, one of whom shares a mother with me, while the other does not. Fifty percent of our X-DNA came to us from our mother in a recombined form. Each of us carries the exact same 50 percent of X-DNA from our paternal grandmother. This genetic package of X-DNA ensures the magic of her ancestral X lines, and the essence of her lineage's divine masculine was given to us by our father. Females are change-makers in X-DNA because they shake up their X-DNA and pass along a random blend, but men ensure a consistent inheritance of their own mother's X-DNA lines in all of their daughters. X-DNA does not stand on its own as an independent test; it is included in autosomal DNA testing. Some testing companies have what is known as a "chromosome browser" that lets you look at comparisons of your own autosomal DNA and X-DNA as shared with another person. This can shed light on shared ancestral lines, as you will only share X-DNA on the inheritance patterns shown earlier in the chapter. Statistically, male/XY siblings could have identical X-DNA inheritance from their mother, or they could not share any at all. Chances are that they will share some X-DNA, however. Female/XX siblings who share a father will always have 50 percent identical X-DNA as the copy of X he passes down to daughters is always the same that he inherited from his own mother. Like their male siblings, females who have the same mother could statistically share an iden-tical inheritance from her, or they could not share any at all, but it's most likely they will fall somewhere in the middle.

Suppression and misunderstanding, purposeful or otherwise, of the sacred feminine and the divine masculine has created quite the political and social divide through history. Women have suffered horribly because of, and continue to fight, the patriarchal norms that deny them equality in nearly every area of life. Men also have their own battle in that they are expected to "be a man" and exhibit most strongly what society deems as masculine behavior, and any expression of the sacred feminine is often belittled or is cause for labeling in a way that is meant to belittle. These norms, along with the massive chasm that now separates us, is not how we were meant to be. Yes, there are physical and genetic differences between XX and XY people, but the ability to truly manifest our innate magic has too long been, and infuriatingly still is, defined by people with financial, political, or religious agendas, or all three. We need the world to change how we view humanity; we need it to embrace the divinity within each person as it naturally manifests. Women/XX people should be allowed to embrace their divine masculine, and men/XY people should be able to express their sacred feminine, all without repercussion or fear. We are each a unique expression of the yin and yang of humanity. We exist on a spectrum, not in extremes, and our DNA is proof of that.

Your Chalice of X-DNA

The magic of X-DNA lies in its inheritance patterns. Like a river, it twists and flows down through the generations in a crisscross pattern, shaking up our genetic composition and carrying a watery magic that, like autosomal DNA, is unique to each person. From this stream of X-DNA, men receive a hefty dose of the sacred feminine from female ancestors, including their direct mother line. Because women also receive an X from their father, they can capture an essence from him that, while not exact to the Y-DNA passed from father to son, nevertheless opens an energetic door to the divine masculine that is carried along the direct paternal line. It also accesses that masculine energy from other male ancestors along the X-DNA lines of inheritance.

This blending of the sacred feminine and divine masculine is necessary to give balance to each person. Even in our current world of horrendous patriarchal oppression and marginalization, we should always do our best to be open to the divine and the sacred within ourselves and in others. In its purest form, each is a necessary ingredient that offers balance to the entirety of being. The masculine is not more, nor less, than the feminine, and vice versa, and neither one can be discarded over the other without creating a significant imbalance. Rather we must find a way to incorporate both energies into our beings and daily life. Being mindful of, and working with, our X-DNA ancestors is a way to tap into the essence of both energies and allow the flow of energy to come to us.

This flow of DNA, and the way we each receive it, has always brought to my mind a chalice. On many magical paths, the chalice represents the element of water, the womb of the goddess, the sacred feminine. It collects this magic and is then able to disperse it via the drinking of its contents, both literally and metaphorically. When we think of our X-DNA as the chalice, we can then open to the ways in which we are each able to partake of the watery, life-giving magic that differentiates us and offers us the essence of the sacred feminine and divine masculine in a way that is suited to our unique physical being. We each, as one of a kind, wondrous individuals, receive into our own chalice the collective magic from the river of genetic inheritance.

Journal Magic: Your X Chalice

You will need your journal and pen, markers or pencils in a variety of colors, and your seven-day candle. Clear the energy of your space with your clearing spray and state the intention that you are creating a love-filled, creative, and self-assured atmosphere. Light your seven-day candle. Open the session in your usual way.

Stare into your candle flame for a few minutes and consider the ancestors from whom you have inherited X-DNA. If needed, use the appropriate X-DNA chart and compare it to your own Tree of Lineage, if you have created one. If not, consider the flow of X-DNA inheritance from your ancestors to you. How might the sacred feminine and divine masculine manifest in you because of them? Does their history have any influence on how you externally represent that inheritance? How about your feelings on the sacred feminine and divine masculine? Do you feel more drawn to one over the other? How might you be more open to either, or both?

Think now on what this chalice might look like for you. Again, this is a creative process, there is no right or wrong. This is a mind's eye manifestation of the positive genetic energies that flow down from the X-DNA ancestors to you, an image that you can conjure to mentally capture that energy and sip from that chalice of sacred divinity. Your chalice is for you alone, as there can be no other in the world like yours because no one else in the world is you!

Write down a description of your chalice. What does it look like? What does it feel like? Are there many colors, or just one? Is it ornate or unadorned? If you are comfortable doing so, draw a picture of your chalice. Remember it just needs to serve as a point of reference for the times you might want to refer to your original thoughts about how it looked and felt to you. As with the cloak and crown, this chalice is constructed of only positive energies, so do not allow the dynamics of negativity that might be present in your life to be part of its construction.

When you are finished writing or drawing, or both, create an image in your mind of yourself holding your chalice. Feel its heft in your hand, picture it full of a delicious nectar of ancestral energy that you can sip as desired, to allow the essence of this magic to flow within you.

Snuff your candle, close your journal session, and clear your space with the clearing spray.

Leaks in the Chalice

The chalice can leak where negative ancestral energies sneak into its weaving. This must be attended to frequently. I consider my own chalice as a part of my magic that occasionally needs mending here and there to keep it looking and working its best. Much as some people might check their protective shields for breaks and then repair them energetically, so too do I assess my chalice for leaks, so to speak. I consider my chalice to be a manifestation of just the positive attributes and qualities of my sacred feminine and divine masculine, and I must do the maintenance work to keep it functional.

As with the cloak and crown, your chalice is an energetic manifestation of the positive aspects of the ancestors whose X-DNA you carry within you. Use your mind's eye image of your chalice as a reminder of the sacred feminine and divine masculine within you, and let it help you to express each in the manner that best suits you.

A Ritual of Consecration and Connection

I have a chalice in physical form that I use to work with my X-DNA ancestors. I use it when I need to do research on those particular ancestors, or when I need to take in a dose of wisdom and want to use a physical process to do so. I didn't mean to have a physical chalice for this, but I coincidentally found one that felt and looked like the chalice I'd manifested in my mind. If you'd like to use a chalice-type vessel for your own ancestor work, here's a ritual of consecration and connection. Normally I don't mind cleansing and using magical tools for various purposes, but I keep my genealogy tools separate. If you're able, I suggest also keeping this chalice strictly for ancestral work so that its energy stays intact and focused on its purpose, which is to connect you energetically, via the contents of the chalice, to your X-DNA ancestors.

Materials:
Chalice, cleansed in the manner of your choosing
Five things you can hold that represent the five elements of Spirit
(Ancestors), Air, Water, Fire, and Earth—I like to use crystals,
in particular amethyst (Spirit), lapis lazuli (Air), blue lace agate
(Water), citrine (Fire), and petrified wood (Earth); you can also
choose to envision each element, which requires only your mind
Moonstone to represent the sacred feminine
Tiger's eye to represent the divine masculine
White taper candle
Clearing spray
Small white altar cloth
Beverage of your choice

Instructions:

Start by cleansing your sacred space with a clearing spray. As you clear, with your mind set the intention of the space to be loving, open, and positive. Arrange the cloth on a solid surface. Place the chalice in the center of the cloth, set the candle to the side that aligns with your non-dominant hand (this is so you aren't reaching over or around a flame while you work), and place the five elemental crystals to the dominant side of your sacred space so you can easily reach them. Hold the moonstone and tiger's eye in your dominant hand and slowly breathe a long breath onto them. This infuses the energy of your DNA into them and serves to make an energetic connection among you, the chalice, and your X ancestors. Place the moonstone and tiger's eye in front of the chalice.

Since my own directional and elemental associations differ from most in the United States in that I connect North with Air, East with Fire, South with Water, West with Earth, and Center/Me/Goddess/Ancestors with Spirit, many will find they need to adjust the ritual to their own personal directional correspondences. I also walk a Goddess-inspired path and use that terminology in many of my own rituals. As with any magic, you should alter it so that it fits your own practice, including changing the words, the materials used, or both. This is your chalice, so mix up the ritual to make it your own in a way that is meaningful to your practice.

Light the candle. Take the chalice in your non-dominant hand, pick up the lapis lazuli with your other hand and place it gently into the chalice, then say:

Goddess of the North,

Mistress of Air,

I consecrate this X chalice

And charge it with your energies.

May it connect me with the ancestors.

Continue to hold the chalice. Pick up the citrine and place it gently into the chalice, then say:

Goddess of the East,

Mistress of Fire,

I consecrate this X chalice

And charge it with your energies.

May it connect me with the ancestors.

Continue to hold the chalice. Pick up the blue lace agate and place it gently into the chalice, then say:

Goddess of the South,

Mistress of Water,

I consecrate this X chalice

And charge it with your energies.

May it connect me with the ancestors.

Continue to hold the chalice. Pick up the petrified wood and place it gently into the chalice, then say:

Goddess of the West,

Mistress of Earth,

I consecrate this X chalice

And charge it with your energies.

May it connect me with the ancestors.

Continue to hold the chalice. Pick up the amethyst and place it gently into the chalice, then say:

Under the loving eye of Goddess,

She of infinite names, She of infinite knowing,

I consecrate this X chalice

And charge it with the light and dark ener-
gies of the celestial consciousness.

May it connect me with the ancestors.

Continue to hold the chalice. Pick up your DNA-infused moonstone and tiger's eye and place them gently into the chalice, then say:

This chalice has been blessed by the energies of the elements

And consecrated to its purpose in the eyes of Goddess,

And now is connected by blood and bond to my X ancestors.

May their wise and positive energies always flow
into its contents, and then into me.

May it be so.

End the ritual in your usual way. Let the candle burn down. Remove the crystals and rinse your chalice as needed, then add your beverage of choice. Sit and sip from your chalice to finalize the bond between it and you. If you like, write in your journal about your feelings, and any research plans and goals you have for working with the energies of your X ancestors.

10

Y-DNA: The Staff

For thousands of years, father and son have stretched the canyon of time.

—Alan Valentine

Y-DNA (also known as Y-chromosomal DNA) is one of two chromosomes that determines whether we will be a genetically male/XY person, and it stands alone as its own separate DNA test. Males/XY people get one Y chromosome from their male/XY parent (their other is an X from their female/XX parent) and this is passed along directly on the paternal line. Females/XX people do not inherit any Y-DNA from their male parent. As with mitochondrial DNA, every few thousand years, small non-harmful mutations will occur in a male's Y-DNA that causes a slight change in the line that then continues to be passed down. These mutations are classed into individual haplotypes, which are then organized into haplogroups, which are then grouped on a phylogenetic tree, which is like a family tree for Y-DNA.

Y-DNA carries a steady, strong powerful magic within it. For millennia, back to the first modern human, men have passed along an exact replica of their Y-chromosomal DNA (with an occasional small mutation) to their male/XY offspring. This tiny bit of chromosome connects them, one to another, father to son, male to male, XY person to XY person, back through the mists of time. Family dynasties, kingdoms, nations, and more have been rooted in paternal inheritance for generations, family surnames are passed along via the male line in many Western, cultures and, for thousands of years, the idea of family has revolved around the male as its protector and provider.

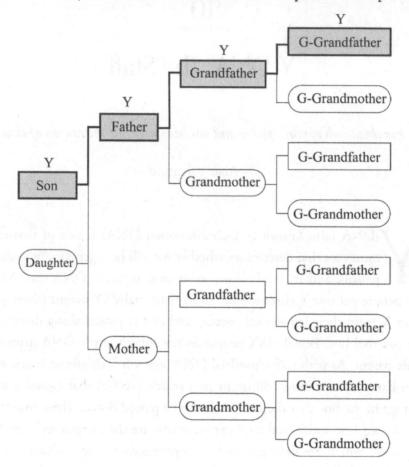

Y-DNA is passed down exclusively from the father/paternal/XY line to only son/male/XY genetic offspring. The direct line of Y-DNA inheritance is known as the *father line* or the *paternal line*.

The Y-Chromosomal Fathers and the Molecular Clock

The Y-DNA fathers are ancient men who represent moments in time. From the singular ancient father whose Y-DNA serves as the source for all humans alive today, to the multiple ancient fathers whose genetic mutations marked a genetic shift for his descendants, we each carry a genetic memory of the power and beauty of their existence. The bloodlines of ancient fathers evolved into distinct groups over the millennia with small genetic mutations that are classed into haplogroups. These form their own sort of tree, much like a family tree.

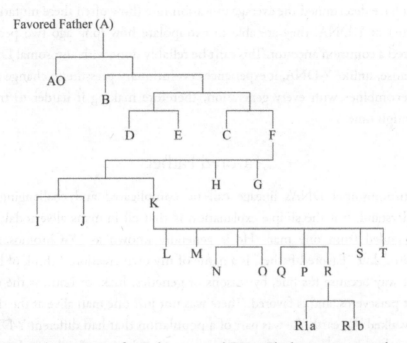

The phylogenetic tree for Y-chromosomal DNA. The letters represent the major haplogroups and the tree shows how they all descend from haplogroup A, which belonged to Favored Father, the common ancestral father for all humans alive today. As the science evolves and more information is discovered, this tree will likely change.

Much like the mitochondrial mothers, the Y-chromosomal fathers appear along a fairly precise path between the ancient father from whom all living humans descend, and ourselves. Scientists are able to approximate when new haplogroups emerged by considering the average rate at which

Y-DNA mutates. Y-chromosomal DNA is passed from male/XY people to male/XY offspring unchanged, save for mutations (tiny, usually harmless, changes) that occur on a predictable timeline. Because of this slow rate of change, Y-DNA provides the information needed for a "molecular clock" much as mitochondrial DNA does. Again, the idea behind this clock is that random mutations add up at a relatively constant rate over time. Since scientists have determined the average mutation rate (how often these mutations occur) of Y-DNA, they are able to extrapolate how long ago two people shared a common ancestor. This can't be reliably done with autosomal DNA because, unlike Y-DNA, it experiences evolutionary pressure to change and it recombines with every generation, therefore making it harder to track through time.

Favored Father

Y-chromosomal DNA's lineage can be complicated and challenging to understand, but the simple explanation is that all humans alive today are descended from one man. He is generally known as "Y-Chromosomal Adam," but "Favored Father" is a name of my own creation. I think of him that way because his line, by reasons of genetics, luck, or both, is the one that perseveres, and is favored. There was not just one man alive at the time he walked the earth, he was part of a population that had different Y-DNA types, but the other types eventually went extinct because the descendants of those other males either didn't have offspring or had only female offspring. Favored Father's particular Y-DNA survived and mutated into the many different types currently found in the world today. Of course, Favored Father, a primitive, ancient man, had no idea that his Y-DNA line would propagate and survive over thousands and thousands of years. Much as Lucky Mother is often conflated with the biblical Eve, so too is Favored Father equated with Adam. As with Lucky Mother and Eve, the common Y-DNA ancestor and the biblical Adam are not the same.

Y-DNA Testing

Unlike the straightforward mitochondrial DNA test for which there is one option, the details of Y-DNA testing can be a bit complicated. In simplest terms, there are three types of tests: Y-STR (Short Tandem Repeats), Y-SNP (Single Nucleotide Polymorphism), which is done in conjunction with Y-STR testing, or after it, and Y-DNA sequencing, in which large parts of the Y-DNA are analyzed.

Short Tandem Repeats

The Y-STR test is what you'll be getting if you choose a Y-37, Y-67, or Y-111 marker test at Family Tree DNA. This test looks at very short segments of Y-DNA along particular sections of the Y chromosome, and how often they repeat. The analysis shows an estimated Y-DNA haplotype, which is a grouping of all the tested markers that characterize the person taking the test. The more STR markers one male has in common with another male, the more closely they are related. Large groups of men who share similar STR markers and a common, ancient, ancestor, are then placed into a general haplogroup. This test is good for looking at early paternal line ancestry.

Single Nucleotide Polymorphism

The Y-SNP test is similar but looks more specifically at single spots along the Y chromosome. Remember the A, T, C, and G nucleotides that hook together as building blocks for DNA? When they replicate, sometimes a typo occurs in the copying of the code. The SNP test is checking for those typos in the A, T, C, and G letter strings of those building blocks. Do you see the typo in the following pattern?

AATGGTAATGGTAAT*C*GT

These typos are usually a normal occurrence and create variations in the Y-DNA. Looking at this information, then comparing it with a baseline, provides what is needed to be more specific about determining on which particular branch of a haplogroup a man belongs. This testing can be done with specific requests based on Y-STR results, but it can be hard to figure out what SNPs are best to test next. If you choose to test with Family Tree DNA, as soon as the initial Y-DNA test results are available, I suggest joining a group on the site called a "haplogroup project." Be sure to choose one that reflects the haplogroup designation, of course. The people who run those groups are very knowledgeable and can guide members to the correct path of further testing. Women who have tested male relatives, or who manage their tests, or both, are also welcome and encouraged to join. I manage Y-DNA tests for my deceased father, my husband, and my grandson, and I'm in groups for all three projects that correspond to their individual haplogroups. Y-SNP testing is good for looking at more recent paternal line ancestry.

Y-DNA Sequence Testing

This test looks at approximately twelve million base pairs of the Y-DNA chromosome and includes identification of both Y-STRs and Y-SNPs. It's a very advanced Y-DNA test that is good for reviewing the most recent paternal line ancestry. For some, it might not be appealing, mainly because of cost, but also because it doesn't always provide value in terms of what is desired as the result. For example, my husband has been tested at this level and has exactly one match: a man in Germany with whom he shares an ancestor from about 2,500 years ago. That wasn't helpful for him regarding genealogy research over the last few generations. On the other hand, my grandson has also tested at this level and has a surname match who also matches him on autosomal DNA, and with that information I was able to determine their shared ancestor, a man who lived in the 1800s. Men who feel they have enough information about their paternal line with the much less expensive 23andMe test might also feel they don't need a detailed breakdown of their Y-DNA genetics. For those who are searching, however, this level of Y-DNA testing can be invaluable in solving mysteries involving paternity along the direct male line, and for male adoptees looking for information about their paternal line.

I believe it is important for males/XY people to do a Y-DNA test, at least at a basic level. At 23andMe, you'll get a baseline idea of where you sit in the Y tree. If you choose to test at Family Tree DNA, do so at the highest level that can be afforded. This testing documents the haplogroup of the paternal line; can sometimes give hints as to a surname history for that line, depending on the test chosen; and can assist with finding distant, and sometime close, cousins along the direct paternal line. It also allows a more personal interaction with the magic of the Y-DNA line.

It's hard to know which test to choose. Testing at 23andMe is at a much lower price (and also provides results on autosomal, mitochondrial, and X-DNA), but again it tends to be very general and is usually limited to an upstream or top-level haplogroup. It's not incorrect, but it's not as specific as it could be, whereas Family Tree DNA's Big Y-700, which is the sequencing test, gives a much more detailed breakdown. It really depends on what you want, though. Some people are okay with simply knowing the general top-level haplogroup, others want more info. Think about your goal with Y-DNA testing and go from there.

My husband's estimated Y haplogroup was R-M269, revealed with an older Y-STR test from National Geographic's Genographic Project (now discontinued) that I bought for him as a present back in 2006. I didn't even know what it was testing, really, but it was exciting for an adoptee like him to learn more about his ancient heritage. As a major haplogroup, R-M269 is very common in men with deep European roots and, while it's nice to know, doesn't tell me too much about his particular paternal ancestry, especially in the more recent centuries. At 23andMe, my husband's assigned Y haplogroup is R-L23, which points to a father line ancestor who was born about 4,400 years ago near the Caspian Sea. This is a more detailed assessment of his Y-DNA because they also look at SNPs which will provide more information. At Family Tree DNA where he's had Y-DNA sequencing done with a Big Y-700 test, his assigned Y haplogroup is R-BY192456.

All of his haplogroup designations—R-M269, R-L23, and R-BY192456—are correct. How? R-M269 is a major branch on the R tree and is detected with Y-STR testing. 23andMe's test, which also looks at Y-SNPs, further places him on the smaller branch of R-L23, which sits on the larger R-M269 branch, but doesn't take the testing any further. Family Tree DNA's Big Y-700 test is the most accurate consumer test to date, and it brings him to the precise twig of R-BY192456 on the R-L23 branch, which is part of the larger R-M269 branch of the R haplogroup tree for Y-DNA. He shares that tiny twig with only one other man who has tested; they share a common paternal ancestor from about 2,500 years ago.

Misinterpretations + Assumptions = Y Trouble

The example of how Y-DNA testing results can look different but be the same shows a potential, huge, problem that stems from misinterpretation and misunderstanding of how haplogroup assignments work. Let's use my husband's three different results as representing a grandfather, father, and son who all take a Y-DNA test. The grandfather does a Y-37 test (Y-STRs) with Family Tree DNA, the father tests with 23andMe (Y-STRs and Y-SNPs), and the son decides to do a Big-Y 700 (Y-DNA sequencing) at Family Tree DNA. They're likely going to show what appear to be different results (and remember, as grandfather, father, and son in a direct line, they're supposed to be identical). The grandfather would show the R-M269 haplogroup, the father would show the R-L23 Y haplogroup, and the son would show the R-BY19246 Y haplogroup. If they didn't know that the son's Y haplogroup designation is a more refined version of the father's, whose Y haplogroup designation is also a more refined than the grandfather's, there might be incorrect assumptions made about paternity along the line that would be a mistake, and that could be destructive and lead to a lot of trouble within a family. I've seen this happen more than once. Many families have been torn apart, temporarily, due to misunderstanding of how to interpret DNA testing results. Thankfully there are online groups that help to set them straight, but I shudder to think of the people who don't reach out and instead assume there's been deceit on the part of a partner that resulted in a misattributed parentage event. The same can happen with autosomal and mitochondrial DNA testing, but it's not something that I've seen to be an issue like the perceived mismatches with Y-DNA.

The short takeaway from this is that you should never make assumptions about DNA test results. If you're not very experienced, check in with someone who *is* very experienced. This is where a genealogy mentor can come in handy, and also a membership in one of the many online groups that focus on genetic genealogy. Additionally, you should always strive to further your understanding of DNA test results and how they apply to you, and others. Not only does this keep the family story in the realm of truths, but also focuses the magic in the right direction.

Your Staff of Y-DNA

From my woman's point of view, the paternal line is a nebulous creature. While I knew that I had given birth to the next generation because I carried each of them within my body, not every man knows when he has contributed to the creation of a new person. I see this reflected all the time in the "genealogy surprises" that pop up in the DNA results of clients. Inevitably, there is an unexpected parent, usually a father, or a sibling that no one knew existed. The ability of men to procreate far exceeds a woman's pace. The most prolific woman in history is Valentina Vassilyev, who is said to have given birth to sixty-nine children in twenty-seven pregnancies. While that seems impressive, it doesn't even come close to Moulay Ismail, emperor of the Moroccan Alaouite dynasty from 1672 to 1727, who is said to have fathered at least 1,171 children. It is thought that Genghis Khan may have fathered between one thousand and two thousand children, and it is also purported that up to sixteen million men alive today, who are living in the regions that Genghis conquered, could be his descendant or that of one of his close male relatives.

The extraordinary power of Y-DNA becomes readily apparent when these statistics are considered. For a very long time, as a woman/female/XX person, I didn't consider that I had access to the magic of Y-DNA. I thought of it as a man's DNA and didn't consider the essence of the divine masculine that is part of me and that has influenced me just as much as the rest of my genetic makeup. In 2007, I experienced fully the power of Y-DNA's magic, thanks to a few words from my father.

I was working as an RN in a very busy inner city surgical ICU. Nursing is a career that demands a lot, both in the physical and mental realms, and nearly two decades of experience at that point had put a lot of stress on my body and mind. On what turned out to be my last bedside shift, a very confused, critically ill patient physically attacked me and caused a grievous injury to my hip that left me unable to walk and in need of surgical repair. During the long months of recovery, I grappled with a wild swing of emotions surrounding the likely end of my bedside career and my newfound mobility impairment. I became very sensitive to perceived negative reactions from others to the very slow rate at which I moved with my walker, and I didn't want to leave my house. I became anxious about finding a parking spot because distance equaled pain, and the exasperated sighs of people who wanted to hurry along but found me in their path were hurtful and I was embarrassed. It became problematic very quickly. I lamented to my father over the phone that I didn't want to go anywhere because so many people stared and made comments about me using a walker to slowly get around. He was sympathetic to my plight but in his usual no-nonsense fashion, laid waste to my pity party. "Who cares? Keep moving," he told me. He then related to me how he was the great-grandson of a man who worked hard, despite limitations, to create a better life for his children. I wasn't convinced, and when I needlessly reminded him that I wasn't a man he patiently replied, "Yes, honey, I know that, but you're the daughter of one."

A few years after this conversation I would find out that his father line wasn't what we thought, but in that moment, his words of pride in the strength of his paternal lineage really made me think. Why wouldn't I be influenced by his Y-DNA? While I technically don't carry Y-DNA from my father, I carry X-DNA that he gave me that holds energy from his mother's male ancestors, along with his autosomal DNA that makes up half of my genetics and carries energy from all of his ancestors. I thought of other things I got from him: bits of my appearance, certain mannerisms, an enjoyment of football, a deep love for his city of birth, Washington, DC, and so much more. Was there a reason why I could not carry the energetic essence of his paternal line magic?

Later in my recovery, as I transitioned from walker to cane, I thought of my father's words—get moving—and that lead to the question of, "How is my magic moving me?" I considered for a long time the negative emotions I felt toward many men, some valid, most likely not, and how I tended to paint them all, save a very select few, with a suspicious brush based on my own experiences with patriarchal oppression and abuse. I always said there was magic everywhere, but my words did not match my actions. I lived fully in the sacred feminine and did not seek the balance that would be provided by accessing the divine masculine within myself. When my grandson was born in late 2008, he, and his potential as a man in the future, provided the impetus I needed to really work on creating a magical practice that was more equitable, and that included all of my ancestors instead of just the female ones with which I'd nearly exclusively worked. During that time, I began to associate my cane with the paternal line influence of my father. His certainty in my ability to persevere was present in that cane as it literally held me up and kept me from falling over as I was walking. My cane became my metaphorical staff of Y-DNA. It represented strength and a literal connection between me and the earth. It provided balance and walking with it reminded me of my father's love, and his faith in my personal power to overcome obstacles. Our relationship had been contentious for many years, but with that "staff" I found that I could feel the energetic connection with him, and with his paternal line ancestors, men who traveled and struggled and worked to provide food and shelter and safety for their families, and who offered the essence of their Y-DNA to their female descendants, if only they would open to it.

Take a moment to consider yourself as the latest in a magnificent father line of men who persevered and thrived, even if it was just long enough to contribute to creating a new life. What strengths do you feel in yourself? How do you manifest this father line in your life? How do you provide balance, strength, and love to yourself? To others?

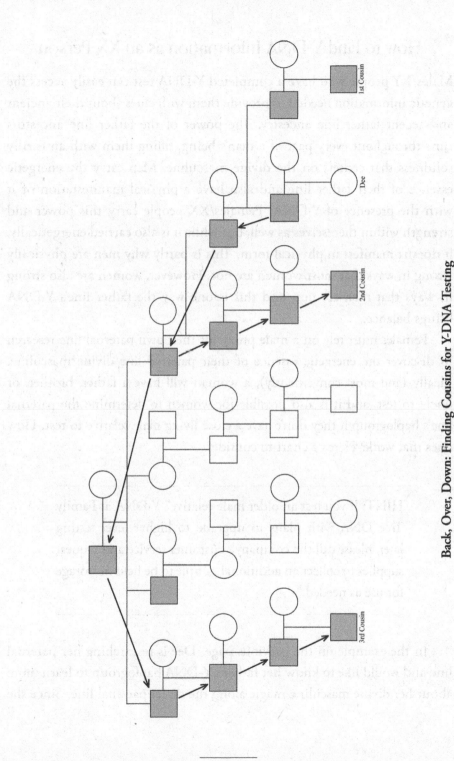

Back, Over, Down: Finding Cousins for Y-DNA Testing

How to Find Y-DNA Information as an XX Person

Males/XY people who have a completed Y-DNA test can easily access the genetic information needed to provide them with clues about their ancient and recent father line ancestry. The power of the father line ancestors runs throughout every part of a man's being, filling them with an earthy solidness that centers on the divine masculine. Men carry the energetic essence of their father line and also have a physical manifestation of it with the presence of Y-DNA. Females/XX people carry this power and strength within themselves as well, but while it is also carried energetically, it doesn't manifest in physical form. This is partly why men are physically strong in ways that most women are not. However, women are also strong in ways that men are not, and this is one way the father line's Y-DNA brings balance.

Females must rely on a male proxy for their own paternal line research to discover the energetic essence of their paternal line divine masculine. Ideally (and most conveniently), a woman will have a father, brother, or uncle to test, and it is also possible for women to determine the paternal line's haplogroup if they don't have a close living male relative to test. How does that work? Here's a chart to consider.

HINT: If you test an older male relative's Y-DNA at Family Tree DNA with plans to upgrade to higher level testing later, please call the company's customer service and request supplies to collect an additional sample to be held in storage for use as needed.

In the example on the previous page, Dee is researching her paternal line and would like to know her father's Y-DNA haplogroup to learn more about her divine masculine magic along the direct paternal line. Since she is female, however, she cannot test Y-DNA because she doesn't have any. She has a brother who could test, but he is unwilling, and both her father and paternal grandfather are deceased. She has an uncle and first cousin who are also appropriate but they are also hesitant. Is it hopeless? No! She can still possibly find a suitable proxy to discover the information she seeks. She can trace her tree back to her great-grandfather and then do a bit of "shrubbing" to add his siblings. In this scenario, her grandfather has a brother who has a direct line male descendant, a second cousin. Also, her great-grandfather has two brothers and one of them has a direct line male descendant, a third cousin.

This is called the "back, over, and down" method of looking for a suitable person to test, and it can also be used for mitochondrial DNA testing if you are looking to discover more about a maternal line from which you don't directly descend, like your father's mother. Just remember, when searching for male/XY descendants to test, there must be an unbroken line of father to son connections.

Journal Magic: Your Y-DNA Staff

You will need your journal and pen, markers or pencils in a variety of colors, and a seven-day candle. Clear the energy of your space with your clearing spray and state the intention that you are creating a love-filled and creative atmosphere. Light your orange seven-day candle. Open the session in your usual way.

Stare into your candle flame for a few minutes and think about your father line. Where did they come from? How far have they traveled over the millennia? What ancient cultures do they represent to you? Recent cultures? If you have autosomal DNA results (like Ancestry), look at your ethnicity estimate. Can you attribute certain bits of it to your father line's ancestry? If you've got a Y-DNA haplogroup designation from 23andMe or Family Tree DNA (or one for your father, if you're female/XX), look at its placement on the phylogenetic tree for Y-DNA. How many major haplogroup mutations have happened in your father line that lead you back to Favored Father?

Do some research online about your (or your father's) Y-DNA haplogroup. Where did it originate? Think about the places the ancient fathers lived during the many lifetimes before yours. How might you represent in your staff these ancient fathers? Your father? Yourself? You can refer to any trees you've created if that helps you create a mental picture of your father line and its roots.

If you prefer not to consider paternal line relatives that are known to you in this lifetime, that is fine. Simply skip past them and move to the ones further back.

Think now on your staff's appearance. As with the cloak, chalice, and crown, this is a creative process. Your staff is an energetic symbol of balance, strength, and fatherly love. As you walk your life's path, this staff serves as a connection between you and the earth, it grounds you, reminds you of your purpose in life, and encourages perseverance in the most extreme of circumstances. It holds the essence of the divine masculine for all of us.

Write down a description of your staff. What does it look like? What does it feel like? Is it heavy or light? What's it made of? Wood? What kind? Is it simple or ornate? If you are comfortable doing so, draw a picture of your staff. It doesn't have to be a perfect drawing; it just needs to serve as a point of reference for the times you might want to refer to your original thoughts about how it looked and felt to you. Remember it is constructed of only positive energies, so do not allow the dynamics of negativity that might be present in your life to be part of its construction.

When you are finished writing or drawing, or both, create an image in your mind of yourself walking with your staff. Feel its heft in your hand, the balance it provides, feel its strength fueling your energy with its ancient father power. Open yourself to the grounding influence of its connection between you and the earth.

Snuff your candle, close your journal session, and clear your space with the clearing spray.

Breaks and Bends

Negative ancestral energies can work their way into the energetic weaving of your staff. Again, this must not be allowed and must be attended to frequently. My energetic staff will occasionally need mending, and I do this with an ongoing process of ancestral healing that is tied to the integrity of my staff. I do not allow negativity to energetically sit within me. My staff is a sacred representation of my father line energies, and I work to keep it clear and clean so that I can use it as a source of balance and strength. Your staff is a positive energetic manifestation of the Y-DNA father's power. Use the mental image of your staff as a reminder that you are carry the energy of the earth within your being, fueled by the ancient fathers.

Honoring the Father Line

Consider this short ritual to pay homage to those in your direct father line. Some paternal lines are flush with information, back several generations or more. Others are vague in that there is only the knowledge that a nameless man was father to a son. Whether you know none, one, several, or many names, take the time to envision and honor the fathers of old.

Materials Needed:
>   Red chime/spell or taper candle
>   Needles or leaves from an evergreen tree
>   A piece of tiger's eye
>   A small cloth bag
>   Journal and pen

Instructions:

Cleanse the energy of your space with your clearing spray. Sprinkle the needles or leaves around the base of your candle. Place the tiger's eye next to the candle. As you do so, close your eyes, quiet your mind, and envision your father line. Names and faces are not necessary, the father line exists within each of us whether we can visualize it or not. If you feel any negativity in the moment, any trials or tribulations, try to lay them aside and simply picture the essence of the fathers moving within you, through you, the ancient and wise flow of the divine masculine driving the force of life through you.

Open your eyes and light your candle. If there are names from your direct paternal line that you'd specifically honor, say them now. If you don't know any names, that's okay. If you'd prefer not to say anything at all and just quietly honor the divinity within yourself, do that. I will use myself and my father line names as the example, and please substitute your own father line names if you know them and plan to speak them aloud:

I light this candle in honor of my known father line ancestors: Theodore, John, Joseph, James, and in honor of those unknown to me by name, all of whose energy I carry within me.

OR

I light this candle in honor of my father line ancestors, whose energy I carry within me.

As your candle burns, sit quietly and think on your connection to your father line. If you've been to the location of the known source of your father line, revel in the memory. If not, imagine yourself there, walking in the same footsteps as these men who walked the earth before you. If you prefer, sink into the grounding energies of earth. Feel your feet on the firm, warm soil, your strong body moving across the land as you head into your future. Your mind and purpose are balanced. Breathe in and breathe out, feel the power of 150,000-plus years of divine masculine move through you from root to crown. You are a much-loved child, a manifestation of ancient father knowing, a genetic drumbeat, pulsating a song of blood and water and fire and earth and sky, uniquely positioned in this world to manifest a destiny of your choosing.

When you are done, let the candles burn down. Gather the needles or leaves and put them into the small bag, along with the tiger's eye. Place them under your pillow and go to bed with the intent that you will dream of the ancient fathers. Be sure to place your journal and pen at your bedside. When you wake up, immediately write down anything you remember about your dream time.

The End of the Line

All people alive today are descendants of Favored Father, however, for the males/XY people who do not father male offspring of their own to pass along their Y-DNA, their personal branch of their Y-DNA line ends. That doesn't mean the haplogroup ends though, only the individual line on which there are no further male offspring. Just as various Y-DNA lines from Favored Father's time slowly went extinct, until his was the only one left with living descendants, they continue to do so today.

Daughtering Out, and the Final Y-DNA Son

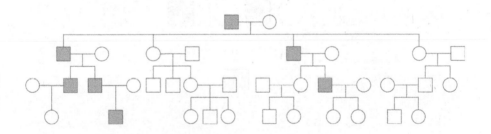

Daniel, and his male/XY descendants, are shown in gray. Of the four children of the original couple, only one of them has a grandchild who carries the Y-DNA of the line. The other three have daughtered out and the Y-DNA line for their line has ended.

I will give my husband as an additional example of a father/paternal line that is ended. Because he fathered two daughters and no sons, there is no male child to whom he has passed his Y-DNA haplogroup of R-BY192456. Therefore, his Y line has "daughtered out." He has four older brothers with whom he shares a father, and they all share the same Y-DNA haplogroup.

One brother did not have children; therefore, he is the final Y-DNA son of his line. One brother has only daughters, therefore his line is also "daughtered out" and he too is a final Y-DNA son of his line. Two of the brothers each have one son. So far, one son has not had children and it is unsure whether he will continue the Y-DNA line or not. The other son has a daughter and a son, so out of the five brothers, only one son has a male descendant line that will continue the R-BY192456 paternal line of my father-in-law. Here's a chart to make things a bit clearer.

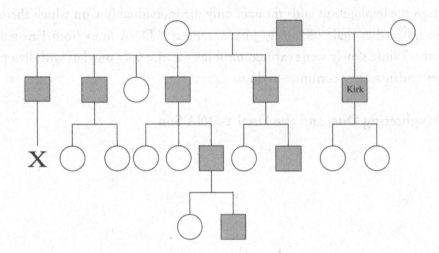

Of course, there are other R-BY192456 males/XY people in the world. We know of at least one—a match in Germany. The ending of my husband's particular line does not end the R-BY192456 line, as it is carried on through his brother's son and grandson. However, you can see how these random endings could eventually wipe a line out of existence. My husband does not have negative feelings about the ending of his paternal line; however, some men/XY people may feel like I do about the ending of my own mitochondrial DNA line, which is a bit sad, or at least have a need to acknowledge it somehow.

To Acknowledge the End of a Father Line

Consider this short ritual to pay homage to those in your direct father line. This is geared toward males/XY people, but females/XX people can do it as well, to honor the ending of the line in their father's stead.

Materials:

Two red penis candles; alternately, use red taper
candles and carve an XY into each one
Anointing oil
Clearing spray
A burning pot or cauldron
A piece of kunzite
A small piece of paper on which you have handwritten
the names of your direct father line ancestors; if you
don't know, write "my direct father line"

Instructions:

Cleanse your space with your clearing spray. Anoint your candles from top to bottom, three times each, and envision the men in your direct father line who came before you. Place the kunzite in the middle of the two candles. Light the first candle and say:

I honor you, recent and ancient fathers of my line, those known to me
by name and those whose names are lost to the mists of time. I honor the
essence of your physical being that lives within me and powers my being.
I honor the sacrifices made that ensured its survival from you to me. I
acknowledge and honor the burden and joy of your life, however brief
or long it may have been.

Light the second candle and say:

I am (or my father is) the last son of this particular father line. I stand
here as a proud representative of all who have come before me (him).
Bless me as I walk my path and do the work that will contribute to the

continuance of other sacred father lines. Thank you for your essence that
powers my being.

Light the name paper and let it burn in the cauldron. Let both candles
burn down. Keep the kunzite next to a framed photo of a male ancestor in
your direct line, or a photo of yourself. Take time to sit with it occasionally
to remind you that your time here on earth provides balance and is powerful
in many ways, and that you contribute to the legacy of men everywhere with
the work you do.

 Add tiger's eye to your genealogy toolbox to
represent the divine masculine in spells, rituals, and
other genealogy work.

11

Energetic DNA: The Aura

Auras are like a signature, each as individual as the person they surround.

—Gina Allan

We are each uniquely made, a randomly generated compilation of genetics passed down to us from the generations that came before us. We are infused with their sacred feminine and divine masculine via different DNA pathways: autosomal DNA, mitochondrial DNA, X-DNA, and Y-DNA. Our inheritance of some of our DNA is random; some of it follows a paternal or maternal line and is passed along as an exact copy, except for an occasional mutation. Over the generations, pieces of inherited autosomal and X-DNA can get "washed out" due to recombination and the randomness that accompanies that process. Eventually we do not carry the physical DNA from many of our ancestors. Think back to the inheritance chart for autosomal DNA. Starting with our parents, we lose about 50 percent of their DNA. Around the generation of our third great-grandparents, we begin to lose inheritance from entire ancestors, meaning that we start to have ancestors from whom we've inherited no physical DNA. From there, we increasingly lose more as the generations get further back. Yet, we are still descended from them. How then, do we explain genetic memory? Why is it that we can feel attachment to these people with whom we don't share physical DNA?

As magical people, we are blessed with minds that are open to the possibilities of the great unknown, of the mysteries that surround humanity, and of our unseen connections via the stream of consciousness from the celestial divine. As such, we can then understand how energetic signatures, much like physical DNA signatures, can be passed along to descendants from their ancestors. I feel these genetic signatures from our ancestors with whom we no longer share physical DNA reside in our individual aura as an energetic form of DNA. While I might not physically carry any genetic snippets from my eighteenth great-grandmother, for example, bits of her energy, and her memory, reside within the aura that surrounds my body. All the DNA we don't inherit from any ancestor, starting with our parents, can be found within the aura as energetic DNA.

The history of the aura is intriguing. In Latin, the word "aura" has a similar meaning in other languages to the words wind, breeze, and breath. Aura is a minor deity from Greek mythology whose name means "breeze." Near the end of the 19th century, "aura" was the word used by spiritualist circles to describe a subtle emanation of energy from the body. The aura, in a form like what we know now, was made popular by Charles Webster Leadbeater (1854 to 1934), a former priest in the Church of England from which he resigned to become a member of the Theosophical Society. He also had some unusual ideas about the origin of men, claiming that some came from Mars, but the smarter ones hailed from the Moon. In 1910, he blended the Tantric chakras into the concept of the aura but didn't acknowledge his sources.

From there, others in the Western world began to reinterpret the aura and the chakras in various ways. American esotericist Christopher Hill presented a modified view of Leadbeater's chakra/aura combination in his book *Nuclear Evolution: Discovery of the Rainbow Body*.[12] In the 1980s and 1990s, the chakras and the accompanying aura became part of the New Age conversation, and it continues today. Many people, including Kirlian pho-

---

[12] Boulder Creek, CA: University of the Trees Press, 1977

tographer inventor Seymon Kirlian, have sought to capture the aura in photograph form, but the technique, and other methods to prove its existence, has not been able to be scientifically reproduced. All in all, the scientific community tends to be skeptical of the aura's existence. Magical people, however, generally are not hesitant to explore and embrace these concepts, and to then utilize them.

I had my first experience with the aura as a small girl. My grandmother read cards at her kitchen table, and I was often tasked with making coffee, and then keeping out of the way until the reading was done. As part of the reading, clients were often brought to the altar my grandmother kept in her hallway, usually to make a petition to Mary, Mother of Christ. I noticed that these people, including my grandmother, seemed to have a glow about them in the darkened space, but I didn't think anything of it because it's just how I saw people. When I mentioned it to her, she told me about the aura and suggested that's what I might be seeing. Since then, I've paid attention to the various colors I sometimes see around people, and when I started working on my own genealogy, realized this energetic field was the obvious place for our non-inherited DNA to reside, and a way for those ancestors to share with us the essence of their wisdom and their experiences, both good and bad.

Levels of the Aura

The aura has seven levels: etheric, emotional, mental, astral, etheric template, celestial, and spiritual. Our energetic, physically non-inherited, DNA resides in all layers. It is diffuse and moves through the various layers as we need it. I find that much of our most recent non-inherited DNA, like the pieces we don't inherit from our grandparents, stays close to our physical body in the etheric layer. The more distant non-inherited DNA, like from a grandparent many generations before us, has moved further into the outer layers. Our most ancient noninherited DNA lies in the furthest reaches of the aura.

The aura also can be seen in varying colors, depending on the energy of the person it surrounds. Colors can be symbolic of different things to each of us. These are a few of the positive associations I have for each color:

- Black—Rebirth, protection, stability
- Blue—Healing, peace, water element
- Brown—Animals and livestock, grounding, earth element
- Green—Fertility, good luck, prosperity
- Orange—Creativity, legal matters, attraction
- Pink—Friendship, heart healing, platonic love
- Purple—Psychic awareness, royalty, self-worth
- Red—Romantic love, courage, passion, fire element
- White—Spirit and spirituality, awareness, higher self
- Yellow—Communication, happiness, air element

Of course, these are my own personal interpretations. Yours may vary. Consider what correspondences and meaning each color has for you and think about how the collective non-inherited DNA from your ancestors can affect your energy and alter your aura's colors. Sit with the colors you see before making a judgment about the meaning. Sometimes black can be a negative color if it's attached to a person who's having dark thoughts or a hard time in that particular life moment. It can also mean that a person has powerful ancestral protection! Red can be a color of aggression, or passionate love. Blue can indicate emotional pain, or healing in progress. White can indicate a refusal to see and accept truths, or a powerful ability to see them. Colors and their spectrum of meaning should be investigated by you and documented as part of your journal for reference purposes.

What is the function of this energetic DNA? I believe it is where genetic memory is stored. We feel the influence of our most recent ancestors because their DNA lies in the auric layer that is closest to our physical body. This could explain why recent collective traumas, like slavery and the Holocaust, have such a strong influence on the immediate generations that follow, and why a traumatic event from sixty thousand years ago doesn't carry the same heavy weight to it, other than how it might have precipitated a behavioral change in the ancient ancestors it influenced over those few generations and how that has been passed along since.

Energetic DNA also allows us to engage with our ancestors, some more easily than others. My grandmother is most strongly present for me because I am the daughter of her daughter. Not only do I carry her physical DNA, but also her non-inherited DNA sits very close to my physical body in energetic form and is easily accessible to me. I find I can connect with more distant ancestors, but it takes a bit more energy and time. I must work a bit harder to still my mind and access those outer layers of my aura so that I can engage with those older ancestors. I am a person who is not great at meditation, however, and others may find it easy to move in and among the energies of their ancestral DNA at all levels.

Envision Your Aura

It is possible to get a glimpse of your own aura, and to touch the energies of the ancestral DNA that resides within it. I find this exercise is best done in a quiet and slightly darkened environment, with time taken afterward to reflect and journal the experience.

Materials:
>*Yourself*
>*Clearing spray*
>*A full length mirror*
>*A white candle*
>*A piece of amethyst*

Instructions:
Cleanse the space with a clearing spray and speak the intention of creating a positive, loved-filled space. Light the candle and hold the amethyst in your

dominant hand. You can be clothed or naked, or somewhere in between, the choice is yours. Let your eyes adjust to the light and as you do so, take in several deep breaths, inhaling positive energy, exhaling negative energy. Feel the amethyst in your hand, powering up your innate ability to reach within your own aura to feel the energies there. Once your eyes have adjusted, do a soft gaze into the mirror. This means you let your eyes go a bit crossed, creating a purposeful blur in the mirror. As you do so, look to the edges of your body for a numinous glow. It might be very faint, but eventually you should see a color or two. Think of your ancestors, both known and unknown. Who comes to mind?

After two to three minutes of gazing, step away from the mirror. Set the amethyst next to the candle. Sit down and open your journal and write about what you saw. What color, or colors, did you see? What ancestors came to mind? What do the colors mean to you? Why might those colors have appeared in conjunction with the ancestors that came to mind? Repeat this envisioning as desired to see how your auric colors change along with the ancestors who come to mind.

Remember that all our ancestors, even the ones from whom we inherited no physical DNA, are the people who are responsible for our existence. We carry them within us as a physical manifestation in our body, and as an energetic presence within our aura. This combination of physical and energetic DNA opens the doors we need to fully access our sacred feminine, our divine masculine, our maternal and paternal lines. We can use it to grow and to heal, and to create a legacy of pride and health for ourselves and our descendants.

12

The Surprise Side of Genealogy

*Life is full of surprises; some are shocking, some are
pleasant. It's all about how you handle it.*

—Jaya Kishori

Unexpected news sometimes brings joy and, other times, hurt and
sadness. Genealogy and DNA testing can manifest deep emotions
from those who swim its depths. Over the years, both within my
own genealogy experience and with clients, I've traversed the spectrum
of feelings in regard to the unexpected that can spring forth from DNA
testing results. In my earliest days of working with genealogy and DNA
testing, I thought my own work of researching and testing to find my
adopted husband's genealogical family had adequately prepared me for
everything that genealogy could throw at a person. In 2014, I was shown
that I was so wrong, and I stood face-to-face with some intense challenges. I know that without my daily magical practice, I'd have been a lot
more lost.

Since maneuvering the shadows within my own genealogy, I've felt
called to help others and have shared in the process with others as they
navigate their own shadow journey within the realm of genealogy. A
daily magical practice can provide a strong framework of support when
we choose to beam a light into places that, when kept dark, can be the

source of dysfunction and emotional pain. I also believe the higher good is served by my telling of my unexpected discoveries as doing so opens a door for others to share their own. This collective telling begins the process of neutralizing the shame that is so often associated with secrets. Shining the light of truth can be painful but it decays the stench of secrecy and lies. This facilitates healing and allows people to move forward within the realm of facts.

For several years, I had a large, well-researched tree and I loved it so. It reflected my heritage of French and Scots-Irish ancestry on my mother's side and was flush with ancestors deeply entrenched in my home city of New Orleans and the surrounding areas. My father, who was born in Washington, DC, and was raised around that area, had reached out to me in 2008, and we'd begun to rebuild our very fractured relationship through the scope of genealogy. After talking with him, I was finally able to put aside the well-intentioned but inaccurate family story that I was told as a child, and was thrilled to explore my Spanish and Jewish roots on his father's side, and the Welsh, Cornish, and English ancestry from his mother's side. I hit a lot of brick walls but also had made a lot of headway on other lines. Like many others know who engage in the work of family discovery, I knew this tree would be a lifetime of continuous work, and I felt very fortunate to have the knowledge I'd acquired.

To go along with my tree and the stories that accompanied my ancestors, I constructed a large ancestor altar and spent a lot of time there. Curiously, I couldn't develop a strong connection with some of my ancestral lines but that didn't concern me, as the dead have their own agenda. I paid homage and moved on. In 2014, after solving the mystery of my adopted husband's genealogical roots, then reconnecting him with his birth mother and members of his birth father's family, I decided to test my own DNA just for fun. When the results came in, I admit I was a bit underwhelmed. I'd tested with 23andMe, which was thought at the time to have the best ethnicity estimate, but my ethnicity chart didn't look like I thought it would. Despite the family story of my Blackfoot ancestry, there was no

Native American ethnicity at all. This wasn't too much of a surprise since I'd gotten a more correct family story from my father that specifically did not include Blackfoot ancestry, but I still wondered where that story originated. The bulk of my DNA was categorized as "broadly Northwestern European." I also noticed, in the DNA matches, there were very few surnames that are common to southeastern Louisiana. I chalked it all up to my father's family roots being from Pennsylvania and New York and decided I would wait for the science to evolve a bit more.

My mother, however, was enthralled by my results and also wanted to test her own DNA. She was always very proud of her French heritage and wanted to explore what DNA testing had to offer regarding it. I ordered a test for her from 23andMe, and she sent in the sample right away. I talked my father into testing as well, but he had issues with the "spit" method of sample collection that is standard at Ancestry. I changed his test to Family Tree DNA so he could use the cheek swab method instead, and he sent in his sample a few weeks after my mother. I had originally intended to test him at 23andMe as well, as I had some brick walls in his research that I was trying to get past, but since he had so much trouble doing one test, I let the others go with a plan to get him to do them later. I would come to regret that decision. I had also expanded my own testing by this point and, in addition to 23andMe, had also tested at Family Tree DNA, and Ancestry, and uploaded my raw DNA data to GEDmatch.

I will never forget the day my mother's test results came in. I got an email notification that the test was done. I was sitting in my car in a parking lot, waiting on my husband to wrap up some credentialing certification testing for his job. I logged into the 23andMe and the first place I looked was the DNA matches. Her oldest brother's son, her nephew and my first cousin, Jason, had also recently tested and was her top match. It took me a few minutes before I noticed the percentage of his shared DNA match to her was only around 6 percent instead of the approximately 12.5 percent usually found in a full aunt/nephew relationship. When siblings share both parents, they are considered "full" siblings, and their respective children are full cousins. When they share only one parent, they are called "half" siblings and their respective children are half cousins. My mother and her five older brothers were supposed to be full siblings; they were raised calling the same two people "Mama and Daddy." Because I was new to genetic genealogy at the time, I did a quick search to double-check the range of shared DNA for a full aunt/nephew relationship. My mother and my cousin Jason did not share enough DNA to fall into that category. I felt nauseated when everything clicked, and I realized this lack of shared DNA pointed to his father and my mother sharing only one parent instead of two. What the test results didn't tell me was which sibling did or didn't share which parent. What it really didn't tell me was how to handle the next step.

When a child is discovered to not be genetically related to the expected father, it's termed a "non-paternity event" or NPE. Some people use the term "misattributed parentage event" or MPE, because sometimes it's the mother who is not the parent expected. (I prefer MPE.) It took me a full day, and hours of research to make sure I wasn't wrong, before I called my mother and explained what was going on. Her excitement at digging through her ethnicity estimate and looking at cousin matches was quickly dashed. She thought I might've made a mistake. I was sure I hadn't, but to appease her I reached out to an acquaintance who is now a nationally recognized expert in the field of genetic genealogy. She quickly confirmed my suspicion that either my mother or her brother was not the child of one of their parents.

Although we knew that there was an MPE afoot, we still didn't know which parent, although we defaulted to her father as most likely to not be the parent expected, as that is the more common scenario. We didn't know whether it was her or her brother that wasn't the genetic child of their father, so I came up with a testing plan to funnel us into an answer. Because this particular brother, Ben, the father of Jason, was deceased for several years, I decided to test two of her brothers, Will and Tom, that were still living, as I wanted to show their connection to each other, and to my mother. I also tested a cousin on their maternal side, Miriam, to act as a control, to show the connectivity, or lack thereof, of all the siblings to the maternal cousin. This would confirm whether the disconnect was maternal or paternal. While the tests were pending, we quietly reached out to the few remaining older family members who might have some knowledge of any circumstance that would've contributed to the scenario our DNA testing uncovered. They were all shocked and denied that it was even possible.

When all of the tests eventually resulted, they each showed the two brothers Will and Tom sharing DNA in the "full sibling" range, but my mother matched both of them in only the half sibling range. The brothers matched my cousin, their nephew, Jason, as full uncles and, again, my mother matched him only in a half aunt range. My mother and her brothers all fell within range of first cousin to the tested maternal cousin, Miriam. The brothers also all matched me in the range of half uncle instead of full uncle, and my cousin Jason matched me as a half first cousin instead of a full first cousin. In short, all of this indicated that my mother was not the genetic child of the man she'd known as Daddy for sixty-four years. I can't even begin to describe the level of her devastation when I called with the results. She was the youngest of six, the only girl, and a "daddy's girl" at that. I immediately knew that I would work to seek out the truth, despite her saying she didn't want to know.

Meanwhile, during my mother's discovery, my father's DNA test results came back. I noticed he didn't have a connection to certain cousins on his father's side that he should have had, and I suspected a situation like my mother's. He wasn't really interested in the results, he'd only done the test to make me happy, and I hesitated to call him to talk about it. Instead, I called one of my sisters and told her that I thought the man our dad knew as his father might not actually be his genetic father. We felt unsure about what to do. Eventually we decided that it would be best to tell him, but first we would sit on the suspicion for a while so I could do more research. Shortly thereafter, my father became critically ill during a diagnostic procedure and died several days later. A few weeks after his death, I asked my cousin Mel, the daughter of his deceased sister, to test. Because Mel's mother and my father were supposed to be full siblings, we should've fallen into the range of full first cousins. We did not, we only shared enough DNA to be half first cousins. Mel also had close matches to her mother's paternal side, which I and my father also should've had, but did not. In short, my father was not the genetic child of the man he thought was his father.

When my cousin Mel's results came back, I was stunned and incredulous. I cackled like a crazy hyena before bursting into tears, because what are the chances that a person would show that both their parents have misattributed parentage? It wasn't until my father's results showed the same MPE scenario as my mother's that it occurred to me that my lineage tree was wrong. It was beyond wrong. It had been decimated, viciously cleaved off at the branch point of both of my grandfathers, taking all their ancestors, and mine, along with them. I was angry and sad that my years of research were for naught, that half of my lineage tree had essentially been chopped away by the double-sided ax of saliva and science. One night, my mother's tears of devastation, and her embarrassment over being a "dirty secret," sent me into a sobbing fit of rage and I deleted my online tree and every trace of the grandfathers and their ancestors from my software, along with burning the accompanying paper documents. It was an ugly scene. It was also an impulsive action I came to regret. I have since been able to recapture a lot of the information but even more remains gone, and I now cannot share with others the information I'd spent years compiling.

To give you a visual of how my lineage tree was affected, on the next two pages is a glimpse before DNA testing, and after DNA testing.

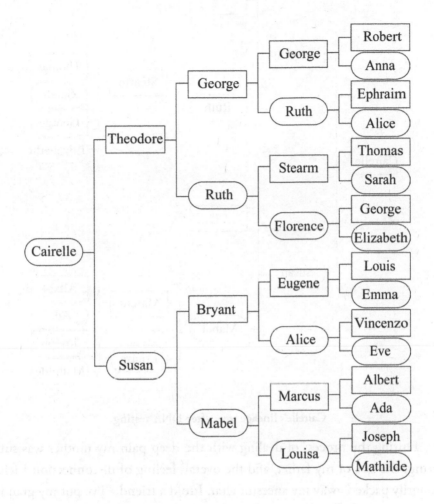

Cairelle's lineage tree, before DNA testing. Most lines go several generations back beyond what can be shown here.

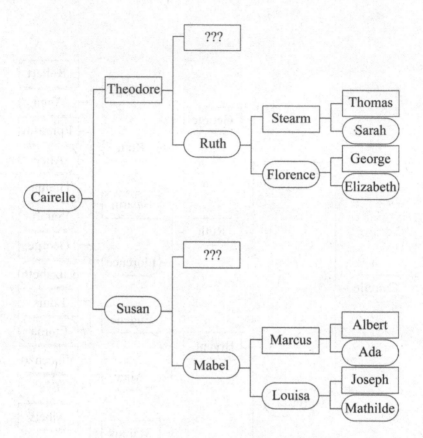

Cairelle's lineage tree, after DNA testing.

During the process of dealing with the deep pain my mother was suffering, the loss of my father, and the overall feeling of disconnection I felt, I angrily packed away my ancestor altar. I told a friend, "I've put my grandmothers in a box in the closet until I'm ready to talk with them again." Looking back, it probably wasn't the best response, or the wisest, as that box rattled and thumped the entire time it was in my closet, but it was what I needed to do at the time. I did my best to support my mother, I grieved my father, and turned to genealogy to solve the mystery of the identity of their genetic fathers, partly to give my mother an answer, and partly because I felt lost without my ancestral practice.

During my time of hard work to discover the truth of my parents' paternity, I went through many emotions: disbelief, sadness, anger, worry, excitement, and relief among them. I turned to my Mirror of Connection nearly daily, hoping to make a connection. I fell asleep at my desk one night and had a dream of hidden ancestors pressing against an opaque veil, asking to "come through." Not long after that, I finally heeded my friend's advice to take my grandmothers out of the closet box and put them back on my reestablished altar in a place of honor. I'd thought for a long time about the circumstances that led them to make the decision to keep their child's paternity a secret and finally concluded that it didn't matter. What did matter is that I loved them both so much, and perhaps what they did was the best choice they could make at the time. Life was very different in the 1940s and women then did not have the options they do now. Once I was able to (mostly) reconcile the anger and move into an acceptance of sorts, I was also able to move forward and continue to work on solving my mysteries.

It took me fourteen months of painstaking daily research to uncover the identity of my mother Susan's genetic father.

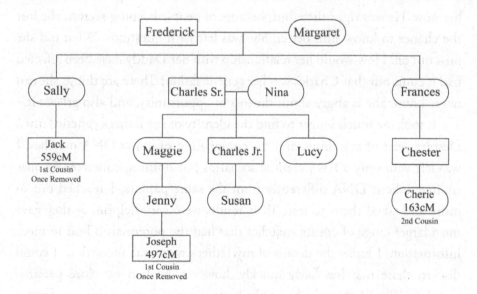

The match to Joseph is what cemented my mother's relationship to her genetic father. There are only so many ways someone who shares that much DNA with someone else can be related to them, and Joseph's match to my mother placed him firmly within the realm of first or second cousin. Coupled with the significant match to Jack, and then to Cherie, and many other matches not shown, I was able to piece the puzzle together and give him a name: Charles Jr. You can see in the tree how the significant matches fit together.

Charles was a brother to one of my grandmother's good friends, and he'd had no other children of which we're aware. My mother was casually acquainted with him. He approached her one day when my sister and I were small girls, fussed over us for a few minutes, then told her, "I was never able to have children of my own; I'd take these two home in a heartbeat." This memory had been lost to her until I told her his name, when it came flooding back. She shared with me that she recalls not thinking much of the encounter at the time, other than he was a kind older man admiring her daughters. We now believe that he knew he was talking to his daughter about his grandchildren, but she had no idea. The memory is bittersweet for her now. He was right there but, because of people keeping secrets, she lost the chance to know him better. She was left with questions. What did she miss out on? How would her relationship with her Daddy have been affected had it come out that Charles was her genetic father? These are things she can never know. She is angry about the loss of opportunity, and also grieves it.

It took me much longer to find the identity of my father's genetic father. Despite years of searching, and the compilation of many DNA matches, I was left with only a few potential scenarios but nothing concrete. Because siblings inherit DNA differently from the same parents, I reached out to mine and asked them to test. Their results were very helpful, as they gave me a larger range of cousin matches that had the potential to lead to more information. I knew the details of my father's maternal ancestry so I could discern those matches fairly quickly, however, he had no close paternal matches. Why? I thought he might be the son of a man who was from a country that did not allow direct-to-consumer DNA testing, and therefore there would be no close matches. My mother thought he might be the son of a military person from another country, since he was born during WWII. Still, the distant matches I did have for him, and for myself and my siblings, pointed to recent ancestral roots in the Ohio and Pennsylvania area. It was confusing, and very frustrating. I eventually accrued enough information to form a few hypotheses but didn't have a reliable way to rank the odds of which was likely the most correct, and with no cousin matches, I could go no further.

Eventually a tool called "What Are The Odds" (WATO) was developed by Jonny Perl, Leah Larkin, and Andrew Millard. WATO is a tool that uses shared amounts of DNA to sort scenarios by probability to then decide which scenario is the best hypothesis (see Resources). My father's case was used as part of its preliminary testing. Leah wrote about my struggle to solve my father's mystery on her blog *The DNA Geek* as part of a series of posts called "Science the Heck Out of Your DNA." The post about my father is number six in the series, entitled "Ted, or When Close Relatives Aren't Available." I'd had such a difficult time with my father's search because, as I'd find out after years of frustrating dead ends, in each of the three generations above him, only one man in each generation would have a child, a son. This left my father with no siblings, and no first or second cousin matches, that could definitively connect him to a particular family.

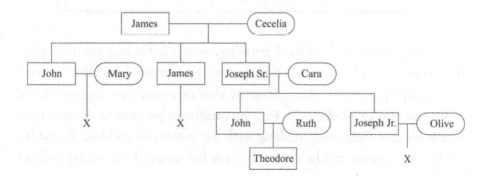

The amazing WATO tool offered enough information to unlock a door to my father's paternal line, along with a third cousin DNA match for my father that emerged and further confirmed my hypothesis. Although anti-climactic, it provided me with a connection to that line, which has proved to be fulfilling, mainly because I felt for a while like I'd never discover the answer to the identity of my father's genetic father. I found myself having to take breaks of a month or more sometimes, just to clear my head so that I could look at the information I did have with a fresh eye. When I eventually reached a conclusion, the relief was overwhelming, and even though he was gone, I was glad to have given myself and my siblings the knowledge of his genetic paternity. I only wished he'd been here for me to share the journey with him. He was a brilliant man and would've enjoyed the challenge!

> Create an infused oil with citrine chips and a preferred carrier oil, such as sweet almond, coconut, or jojoba. Scent as desired with essential oil. Keep it in a small bottle, perhaps with a roller top. Use it to anoint a candle, light it, and let it burn while you do the work of discovering where DNA matches fit in your family tree. You can also set citrine next to your orange seven-day work candle. Hold it in your hand to infuse it with the intention of making connections.

During those years of hard genealogy work, it became glaringly clear that using the tools and other resources we have at hand are an important part of solving mysteries. I turned to my altar every day, opening my Mirror of Connection to ask for help, lighting candles in petition to the ancestors to ask for their help, and speaking with my matroness goddess, Brigid, to ask her for support and help, and to shine her sacred flame on my path of discovery.

If you find yourself on the surprise end of an unexpected DNA match, take a deep breath. While the initial moments can be distressful and uncomfortable, eventually a balance of sorts will be reached. I admit that might take a while. First, you need to make sure you're actually seeing an unexpected surprise and not a mistake in your interpretation. Those mistakes do happen and can wreak havoc, so double-check! Reach out to a mentor, or to an online group to have someone experienced go over your match. Second, try to remember that family is made up of imperfect humans who make mistakes. It's been the norm for secrets to be kept, but thankfully that is changing. If you are the one who discovers a family secret, walk gently and with compassion for all involved. If it's a discovery that changes things for you, treat yourself with a tender hand. It can be a difficult journey. Last, remember the person on the other end of the match may be experiencing similar emotions. There is someone there with feelings, so again, be gentle, be compassionate, be open-minded, follow standards and guidelines. I believe we all want to exist within the realm of love and acceptance. Be the person who helps makes it so.

13

Ancestral Healing

When we heal ourselves, we heal the past, the present, and the future.

—Steven D. Farmer

Ancestral healing can be an important part of genealogy magic, and very helpful in manifesting a more positive life path of one's own. When we work to consciously adjust our personal narrative and then dismantle and unravel the patterns of limiting, inherited beliefs and behaviors, we and our entire lineage evolve. The work of actively healing our lineage is often not comfortable, convenient, or easy, but it's a necessary part of creating a truly healthy and fulfilling life. On a familial level, a regular practice of ancestor work can help to mend intergenerational patterns of family dysfunction, limiting beliefs, and coping patterns. When we work with spiritually vibrant and loving ancestors, it may come to pass that we will better understand and transform patterns of pain and abuse, and gradually reclaim the positive spirit of our ancestral family. This will then work to initiate and potentiate healing breakthroughs, including the establishment of healthy and appropriate boundaries with living relatives for whom we cannot find a remedy for dysfunction. On a collective level, the ancestors can be powerful allies in transforming historical trauma relating to race, gender, religion, war, emotional, physical, and sexual abuse, and other types of pain that affect groups of individuals who have it in common.

Since genealogical family is the source of our physical being and the reason for our existence, it seems sensible that they'd be the first in line to protect us and keep us safe, and to actively keep us from harm. Sadly, that is not always the case, and being related by blood doesn't mean those people will act in our best interest. There are so many circumstances with genealogical, living family that can cause deep emotional pain. Some adoptees may feel like they were unwanted at birth and that's why they were surrendered, or perhaps they've been rejected by genealogical family when they've tried to make contact, which can cause them to feel unworthy. Others are ejected from their family circle due to their spiritual preference, their choice of partner, their sexuality, their affirmed gender. Some parents turn away when the other parent is emotionally, physically, or sexually abusive, or all three. When we descend from people who've done terrible things, or from people who themselves have been the recipient of some sort of trauma, this energy carries itself down through our physical DNA and the genetic memory of our energetic DNA, even if we've never met these ancestors in person. This can perpetuate a negative pattern that continues into the present.

Prior to DNA testing, one adoptee shared with me his feelings of disconnection. He described himself as "probably Latino" but he wasn't sure and, despite having two loving adoptive parents, never did feel like he was truly a part of white American culture. His ethnicity estimate showed him to be around 48 percent Mexican with a focused genetic community connection to a specific location within Mexico, and the other 52 percent was a mix of Irish, English, Scottish, a bit of French and German, and some trace percentages in a few other areas. From that, I hypothesized he probably had one parent of Northern European descent and one parent of Mexican descent. With his permission, I was able to use his DNA matches to identify his genetic mother fairly quickly, and I found close relatives whose ancestors' online records showed movement between their home in Mexico into the United States, and back again, as they traveled in and out for work. As of this writing, he is not interested in going further with his search and has no plans to reach out to his genetic mother or have me continue the search for his genetic father. Instead, he is spending his time exploring his newfound Mexican heritage and this in itself has been very healing for him.

In another scenario, an acquaintance described to me her hesitation to submit a DNA test to Ancestry. She is a Black woman with a family story that includes enslaved ancestors on some branches of her tree. She didn't feel that genealogy had much to offer her. As a white person, I cannot speak to the experiences of Black people within the realm of genealogy. What I can do is read, and I am a big fan of genealogist Shannon Christmas. In a three-part series entitled "Ancestry.com IS for Black People: The True Story of How to Research African American History"[13] on his *Through the Trees* blog, he shares this bit of wisdom:

> To activate the full revelatory power of genetic genealogy, con-
> struct, compare, observe, and record patterns among the pedigrees
> of one's DNA matches. These patterns represent the molecular
> footprints of your ancestors. Follow their lead. Remembrance is
> resistance, restorative justice reversing systematic erasure. Forget
> The 1870 Brick Wall. Seize the opportunity to rise above the
> social media noise and amplify the whispers of your African
> American ancestors. Reclaim their names. Recount their stories.
> Remember their legacy. Ancestry.com is for black people.

I shared these words with my acquaintance, who ultimately did submit a DNA test, and she was quite moved by the ethnicity estimate results. While the work of searching is quite difficult for her so far, she is determined to find success. She has been able to connect with supportive and knowl-edgeable DNA cousins, a network of sorts in which she is finding support for her journey and healing through discovery of her roots.

---

[13] Through the Trees: *https://throughthetreesblog.tumblr.com*

In my own family lines, I descend from multiple slaveholders, some of whom were fairly prominent. Several are mentioned in a case brought before the Arkansas Supreme Court that mentioned that enslaved persons inherited through an estate could be used to pay off debts. Another ancestor of mine was purported to be a murderer and that is why he fled France and came to New Orleans. There is a history of sexual abuse that runs down multiple lines in my family, as well as emotional and physical child abuse. My grandparents lived through the lean times of the Depression. Women were expected to marry and raise children; college attendance was not encouraged and was actually frowned upon. Alcoholism is also rampant. These are all cycles that were not broken before my conception. My physical DNA, and my energetic DNA, and the genetic memory it carries, were loaded with trauma and dysfunctional patterns from the moment I was born, even though I was born to parents who wanted me, and who loved me. I am far from alone in living a life that has the cloud of ancestral trauma hanging over it. I'd venture to say that most, if not all, people carry some. It's not always obvious, of course. For many years, I'd have argued that I was just fine, with many good times, navigating the usual ups and downs. The reality was that I'd be in the midst of living my happy life and then suddenly something would trigger me, and I'd be mired in a sludge of bad feelings for which I could not seem to pin down the source.

These ancestral wrongdoings can also leave an ugly energetic signature on a family tree as a whole and it's not uncommon to see entire family systems embroiled in patterns of physical and emotional abuse or engaging in other activities that point to historical or collective trauma. Dysfunctional family dynamics can perpetuate through generations. "Hurt people hurt people." That's the old saying, and families sometimes seem intent on causing pain for those closest to them. Why? That fact confused me for a very long time, until I began to consider how I carry past trauma from ancestors and current trauma from my parents and grandparents, and the energy from past misdeeds and trauma that affected the generations who lived and died before I was born.

Many people don't recognize that their trauma is a pattern of dysfunction that can stem from people who died before they were born or, when they do see it, they've already engaged in behaviors that have caused harm. Historical trauma is real, and its effects can echo through generations of descendants. How is this possible? We can look to studies on epigenetics that have provided in-depth insight into how trauma can affect not only the people to whom it happened, but also affect their descendants. One study done on mice that had them associate the scent of cherry blossom with a painful shock to the foot showed that not only did the mice who were shocked exhibit distress when they smelled the cherry blossom scent, but also their children and grandchildren who had never been shocked. Children who were conceived during a famine in the Netherlands in the 1940s have higher rates of diabetes, heart disease, and other conditions. It's thought that the physical stress of starvation caused changes to gene expression, or to the genetic on/off switch, that controls those diseases. This change to how the gene turns on and off—with there being no change to the gene itself—was passed down to the children of the people who experienced the famine. Researchers have proposed that DNA methylation—a reversible chemical change to DNA that usually blocks the transcription (copying) of a gene without altering its sequence—explains the way this trauma is inherited. It is important to note that these studies do not prove that trauma is inherited, but they do present a strong case for it. Further studies are ongoing.

People who aren't family, yet who surround us daily, can also cause harm. Consider coworkers and bosses that wreak havoc in the workplace for no good reason. If a woman has a boss who routinely sexually harasses her, and she then conceives a child while she is working in this hostile environment, there is a chance that trauma may affect the child's gene expression for certain diseases. It is certainly carried in the energetic DNA. Most of us have likely heard stories about, or have directly experienced, leaders within our own magical communities who have caused real harm with their bad behavior. People who are emotionally battered often then exhibit their own negative behavior as a result. Perhaps they have children at home who experience stress and therefore will carry that within themselves and pass it down, or they have a coworker that they treat poorly while under stress, and that causes harm to them and those around them. It's a vicious, bitter, and near-endless cycle. There are many ways that trauma can be experienced individually from outside sources that can then cause harm to the family.

So what do we do with this information about inherited trauma? First, knowledge of it helps us to see that people who were affected by trauma in their own lives, and whose ancestors passed down trauma from their own generations, can perpetuate these patterns with their own children and grandchildren, and with others who surround them. Think about someone who has hurt you. Were they also hurt somehow? It's easy to think, "I don't care if they were hurt." However, if you can imagine that the hurt done to you was influenced by a legacy of negative behaviors and pain, it won't necessarily make you feel better, but it will give you a sense of why. I do know that those in my family who have caused me pain did themselves also experience trauma as children and young adults. It doesn't make excuses for what they did, but it provides me with a bit of rationale as to why they might have been set on their path.

However, it needs to be said quite firmly that, despite our individual and collective traumas, both experienced within our lifetime and those inherited from ancestors, as adults we are 100 percent responsible for our own actions and how we treat ourselves and others. Possessing individual and collective trauma does not relieve us of responsibility for the ways we act out and possibly cause pain, and it doesn't mean we should not do the hard work of reaching out in an attempt to heal relationships with those to whom we ourselves have caused pain.

There is also the truth that some people are just horrid, and, even if they knew how to heal themselves or mend a relationship with someone they've hurt, they'd choose not to do so. Instead, they continue to cause harm to others with a brazen lack of integrity and authenticity. They don't care if they shun an adoptee looking for roots, or that they lack feelings of regret for ejecting a gay child from the family unit and leaving them untethered in the world. They will not acknowledge the continued harm of slavery. They refuse to consider that their words and deeds will create ripples of negativity throughout an entire spiritual tradition. While we cannot make these people acknowledge their own role in perpetuating trauma, we can choose to do the needed work within ourselves to deal with our own feelings and the repercussions we experience as a result of their behavior, and we can act as an example to those around us.

It's up to each person individually, then, to assess and then address their own ancestral healing. This does not mean you have to put yourself at risk, emotionally, or physically, by spending time in the presence of people who have caused you harm. What it does mean is that you assess family patterns for individual and collective trauma, and you work on yourself so that you don't perpetuate these harmful patterns. In short, you want to break the cycle. Even if you choose to live only within the circle of your Tree of Influence, it is still important to remember that your own unhealed trauma can affect the people who sit within its branches too, and that in turn can have a generational effect on its own. Another important thought to consider is the effect that active healing can have on how trauma perpetuates its malignant pattern. Remember the mice who were shocked when they smelled cherry blossoms and then passed along their fear to their offspring? After they produced those offspring who inherited their fear, the mice were then allowed to smell the cherry blossom scent without being administering a shock. Over time, these mice lost their stress response when they smelled the scent and were then able to produce offspring that did not have an innate fear of the scent. In essence, they experienced trauma and passed along that fear to their offspring and were then healed of their trauma in such a way that it did not affect their later offspring. If trauma can be healed in mice, then certainly we can adjust our own lineage by manifesting a healing change for ourselves!

There is no one-size-fits-all approach for ancestral healing. For some, it's an easy and straightforward process. For others, the work of healing can cause its own trauma. I am not a licensed mental health professional and therefore cannot, and do not, offer medical advice. To be 100 percent sure that the path you seek to walk toward healing is the right one for you, please seek guidance from a licensed mental health professional prior to undertaking this work.

There's a quote widely attributed to Bert Hellinger about the black sheep-type people in each family:

The so-called black sheep of the family are, in fact, hunters born of paths of liberation into the family tree. The members of a tree who do not conform to the norms or traditions of the family system, those who since childhood have constantly sought to revolutionise beliefs, going against the paths marked by family traditions, those criticised, judged and even rejected, these are usually called to free the tree of repetitive stories that frustrate entire generations. The black sheep, those who do not adapt, those who cry rebelliously, play a basic role within each family system, they repair, pick up and create new and unfold branches in the family tree. Thanks to these members, our trees renew their roots.

Your work to eradicate toxic familial patterns, while it can be difficult, is also valuable and essential.

My own journey to ancestral healing had many twists and turns. For years I functioned—sort of—through some really unhealthy and limiting beliefs, both about myself and the world as a whole. I spent too much time crying over the past and worrying about the future instead of living in the here and now. I read something recently that spoke of a heart that lives in the past and spends time looking at and lamenting over old photographs, and a brain that is so anxious about the future that every day is spent reading tea leaves to predict what is coming. That was me, and I missed a lot of life that way. I spent two decades of adulthood halfheartedly trying to fix what was broken within me but never quite got it accomplished. My inability to see how dysfunctional family patterns and dynamics kept me from reaching my full potential was a barrier to living with full purpose.

When I was forty, I suffered a debilitating work injury that resulted in a surgical repair to my hip and ended my ICU nursing career. I also had another major surgery the same year that left me with disfiguring scars on my neck. In addition to being in physical pain with limited mobility and hating my own reflection, I was also an emotional mess. A dear friend kindly but firmly pointed out how sometimes our mind and body will find a way to set fire to our perception of a comfortable existence to spur us into stepping onto the conscious path of intentional living that we are meant to walk. His words stung, but he wasn't wrong.

During the earliest years of my own work of ancestral healing, I was fortunate to have had an ongoing relationship with a licensed therapist, and she supported me in an important way. Her guidance was invaluable and kept me on a straight path when instead I might have veered in a direction that could have had negative consequences. The work wasn't, and still isn't, easy. It's forced me to stare down ugly legacies, like having slaveholding ancestors, a poverty mindset, women being considered less than men, and a long line of physical, emotional, and sexual abuse. The work has also made me grow as a person. I learned to sit with the energy passed along to me, and to then adjust it in such a way that it resulted in positive actions that are now being passed down to my own children and grandchildren. By sharing some of them with others, I also potentially influence those people into creating positive change, and therefore I also sit on someone else's Tree of Influence. The work we do to heal doesn't affect only us; it affects everyone around us.

It is also important to note that even the most dysfunctional families also have strengths and good behaviors. The mere fact of a person's existence means their ancestors survived well enough to create, gestate, and birth a child who stayed healthy enough to grow to adulthood and then have their own descendants. Families with strong religious or political beliefs who use that as an excuse to turn out a family member for not believing the same, or for not adhering to the tenets of a belief system, may also do things like contribute to food pantries, care for an elderly neighbor's lawn, or coach little league sports. It's likely that less than savory ancestors also had some positive attributes and behaviors. While those good behaviors do not negate the dysfunction that perpetuates the family dynamic, they do speak to an energy that can be harnessed and used in the healing process. I do believe there is a spark of goodness in most people and that is helpful for me to remember when I am working on transmuting the negative energy from my own family and ancestors.

Journal Magic: Family Patterns

To begin your own journey of ancestral healing, you should first start by evaluating yourself and your family for patterns that you think might contribute to negative behaviors in your own life, as well as the positives and strengths that contribute to how you move through life. Cleanse your space with a clearing spray, grab your genealogy magic journal, and light your orange candle.

You may want to open your Mirror of Connection to ask questions, or to receive messages to your subconscious that will remind you of areas that you may want to consider as needing to be healed or realigned. Remember to firmly open and close your Mirror session! Also, refer to your family trees and family story to serve as a reference as you ask and answer the questions that will serve as a guide to the path you will walk during your healing work.

Think about, then write down, the answers to these questions as best as you're able. For those who have little to no knowledge of any genealogical family, this activity may be more difficult to complete. If you want to try, consider opening your Mirror to ask for guidance. Contemplate the questions then write your thoughts on which of your own positive and negative behaviors might stem from family strengths or an inherited familial dysfunction, or acquired from the people who raised you.

- What negative energies do you sense within your own living (or recently deceased) family? What negative life events occurred that might have had an impact on the way they interacted with others?

- What negative life events occurred in the lives of your ancestors? For example, someone who lived through the Depression may have carried the wounds of being hungry, which may have led to behavior patterns later that had a negative effect: hoarding, issues surrounding food (overeating, binge eating), fear of a low balance in a checking account, and so forth. These harmful and self-limiting behaviors could easily have been passed to children.

- Are there stories surrounding any ancestor who may have engaged in negative behavior? Are there family rumors that talk badly of an ancestor? This rumor doesn't necessarily have to be true, nor do you have to think badly of the ancestor, but consider how the potential of their behavior may have affected your family story to the point that negative behaviors evolved. I have a great-great uncle that my grandmother spoke of, and I consider him to be the source of her fear surrounding the possibility that her daughter would be sexually abused by other male family members. This was a prevailing fear all through her life and is one she passed along. I grew up with the belief that most men would try to sexually assault me in some way. I actually did experience sexual abuse at a young age, but I know now that the majority of men are decent and kind and do not seek to engage in inappropriate sexual behaviors with children or with adults who are not interested in a sexual encounter or relationship.

- What strengths lie within your living (or recently deceased) family? What about your more distant ancestors? Are there stories of them overcoming, persevering, surpassing expectations? Think about the good behaviors that might have contributed to the positive energy that lies within each family and person and write those down.

- What negative behaviors do you see in yourself that might be attributed to family dysfunction or generational trauma? For example, I was told repeatedly between the ages of eight and twelve that I was "fat." Looking back on photos, I see now that I was an average girl going through the changes of pre-adolescence and then puberty. My body was changing in the regular way. However, I took this negative language into my subconscious and despite being very fit and healthy through my teens and into adulthood, carried a horrible self-image and low self-esteem. I still don't know the motivation of the people who said that to me, but what I do know is that I have done work to heal the little girl part of me who felt unworthy of acceptance.

- What strengths do you see in yourself that you feel might come from your family? Your more distant ancestors? I come from a long line of women who traveled and survived. The women in my known mother line did not have an easy life. I feel that my ability to persevere, and to thrive during hardship, is a strength that comes from the women who came before me. Despite our tumultuous and fractured relationship, I still say, "I got my brains from my dad." He was riddled with demons and made some poor choices, and he was also a brilliant man who had an aptitude for and a love of learning.

- What else comes to mind when you consider yourself, your living and recently deceased family, and your long-gone ancestors? Are there collective traumas, like slavery or the Holocaust, that bear consideration when you review your family's history? What about your ancestors further back? Where are they from? Did they travel long distances? If so, why? What might life have been like for them?

If you feel emotionally stressed or overwhelmed at any time while doing any of this work, you should stop immediately, close the session, and engage in an activity that is calming. Call someone for support as needed, and don't be afraid to reach out. The process of ancestral healing can be a lot to manage. Some people, like me, need guidance from a professional so please do seek that assistance if you think it's needed, and if you're able. At minimum, you should share with someone that you're working with healing ancestral wounding in your family and that you might occasionally need to talk.

Take some time to read over your entry. It is probably lengthy. How does it make you feel? Do you see patterns of trauma and dysfunction that could influence your family's dynamics? How about the positives? The strengths? It's sometimes hard to see the good things in our genealogical family, but it's most likely that you also are part of one that had, and has, innate goodness and strengths within its structure.

Daily Meditation

At the base of every practice is usually a daily engagement with it that supports our mindful participation. It can be uncomfortable, at minimum, to engage in a healing practice and keeping balance is essential. One way to manage this is with a daily meditative session to stay grounded and remind us of the power of perseverance we carry at our core, despite negative ancestral patterns.

A Quick Clearing Meditation

Sit quietly, feet firmly on the floor, arms relaxed, eyes closed. Picture your body as an extension of the earth and its pure energy. Breathe in and out slowly and deeply. The goal is to feel as relaxed as possible. Consider in your mind that your skin is a sieve, with tiny holes that allow energy to move in and out. With each inhale, picture positive, uplifting energy moving into your body. With each exhale, picture negative energy and thoughts moving out of your body and being carried away to never return.

It may also be worthwhile to keep a daily journal for recording only good thoughts about yourself. Fill it with your positive attributes, your good deeds, your actions of value for others. There is something good in each of us and I challenge you to write about yours every day. Our ancestors gave many of us some heavy baggage and they also infused us with many strengths and excellent qualities.

Work with Singular Ancestors

A friend once shared with me the painful rejection by their mother when they were a young adult that resulted in a decades-long estrangement that was not rectified before her death. While the chance to mend the relationship while both were in their physical incarnation ended when she died, they have since developed an ancestral relationship with their mother on a spiritual level. It has a different dynamic. They feel their mother's spirit has evolved since her earthly time, and she now fully understands and accepts them. There has been healing that has adjusted the lineage, which has likely lessened further inheritance of pain from the friend to their partner, children, and others who feel influenced by them.

Sometimes past issues will not be remedied. I am the fourth great-granddaughter of a man who was an enslaver. He was also the patriarch of a family that has a large descendant tree. I am one of hundreds. After working with him a few times, I feel like the spirit of this ancestor does not feel regret for his actions during his life and there's nothing I can do about that. What I can do is continue to work with the dysfunction and try to adjust the lineage with my own actions. In this scenario, I have made it a point to work with descendants of enslaved persons, especially those who share DNA with me. It doesn't change the past, but it creates a new, positive, energy in the present. Ancestral healing can take a lifetime. The important thing to remember is that by acknowledging the negative pattern and doing the work to transmute it, you have already taken a huge step onto the healing path. That alone creates its own positive ripples for you and those around you.

To Work with a Singular Ancestor
Materials:
> *Photo, copy of signature, or written name of ancestor*
> *Green candle, type of your choice (chime/spell, taper, seven day)*
> *Amethyst, for protection and amplified psychic connection*
> *Mirror of Connection*

Instructions:
Set out a specific time to work with this ancestor and, depending on the energy you experience, consider limiting your time by using a timer to set boundaries for the session length. Cleanse your space with a clearing spray and mindfully set the intention of your work. For example, you might say, "I will manifest a healthy and positive spiritual connection with my deceased paternal grandmother." Place the photo, signature, or written name of the ancestor under the candle, and set the amethyst next to them, in your work-space. Open your Mirror of Connection, then state that you are interested in creating a positive atmosphere and are only receptive to healthy and healing messages and energy.

It can be handy to keep your journal nearby for recording any thoughts that come to mind. Consider how you might develop a relationship with this particular ancestor. What are ways you can manifest their energy in the world in a healing way? For example, in keeping a connection with my paternal grandmother who was a very creative sort artistically and musically, I ask for her for ideas and guidance when working with either of those mediums. Our relationship while she was living was distant at best, but now I find great pleasure at the thought of her when I paint with her in mind. She lives on just a bit in my creativity.

When you are done with each session, be sure to mindfully close it and put the Mirror in its covered place.

My Favorite Herb for Genealogy: Balm of Gilead

Balm of Gilead is an ancient sacramental herb. The tears (or buds, as some prefer to call them) are used magically for healing, protection, consecration, divination, and attracting spirits. These are all applicable to genealogy magic in one way or another, but my favorite use for Balm of Gilead when it comes to ancestral work is healing. There is always a discussion regarding the various sources of Balm of Gilead tears. In this book, I am referring to the resinous winter buds of *Populus x jackii,* a hybrid Balm of Gilead tree that results from a cross between poplar and cottonwood trees and is native to North America.

Balm of Gilead can help to soothe painful feelings surrounding broken relationships. Many of us have lost a loved one with whom our relationship was fraught with hurt and anger, or maybe even abuse, while they were alive. Although we are never obligated to engage with these ancestors, it can be of immense benefit to us if we do healing work, or at least connect, so we can speak words that need to be said and heard.

If you want to address past contentious relationships, place buds around a photograph of that particular ancestor. (If you don't have a photo, write their name on a piece of paper and use that instead.) Write down grievances and hurts about your relationship with this person. It can be long or short, vicious or polite, brief or detailed, and filled with any kind of wording or language that helps you to release some of your feelings. Safely burn the paper then mix the ashes with Balm of Gilead Tears oil, or another oil of your choosing. Anoint a candle with the oil/ash blend, then light it near the picture of your Ancestor. Make some tea, have a seat, engage in a conversation. Say the things you need to say. The candle color can be of your choosing, but I like white for ancestral work, and I might also use blue in this instance for my own peace and healing. Pink could be another option as it represents love, which in this scenario, would be love for myself and taking care of my own emotional upset. A black candle for protection is a consideration as well, depending on your circumstances. One or more candles is fine, depending on what you feel you need. This is your work; you frame it to your preference. When you're done, or if you find that you are very uncomfortable, end the session with thanks and a firm "Goodbye!" Snuff the candles, cleanse your space with a fragrant herb or spray, take a shower and picture your hurt and anger rolling off and away from you, and down the drain. If you prefer other cleansing, do that. You can do this work once or repeat as necessary for as long as you need. Be sure you firmly close the session each time and do a space and personal physical cleansing.

Balm of Gilead can also be a salve for the broken-hearted. When we lose people who are very dear to us, the pain of living with their loss can be quite distressing. Balm of Gilead can help to soothe this ache. Write the person's name on a bud and anoint it with a tiny bit of oil, then carry it with you in a pocket or purse. Touch the bud when you want to feel connected, send love, receive love, and remind yourself that you and this person spent your time together in happiness. You can place the bud in something small that belonged to your loved one—a coin purse, a handkerchief—and keep that with you. You can also use the buds, anointed candles, and a photograph to connect. Write a letter if you like. Sit and visit. Bring tea and a treat and be sure to share your food and drink with your ancestor by leaving a tiny amount on the altar. When it's time to end, thank your ancestor for the visit and say goodbye. To clean up your offering if you shared one, compost it or leave it outside, if it's a safe food for animals. (For example, don't leave chocolate, as it may be ingested by a dog.) There is an animal who will certainly appreciate the snack.

Additionally, you can crush the buds and mix with herbs of your choice to create an incense. A suggestion would be rosemary for remembrance or lavender for protection. Burn as needed whenever you want to connect with an ancestor.

Balm of Gilead Tears Oil

If, instead of buying, you prefer to make your own Balm of Gilead Tears oil for magical use, this is a basic recipe:

1. Fill a small jar nearly to the top with buds.

2. Pour olive oil into the jar until the buds are completely submerged.

3. Cover the jar top with a paper towel and secure with a ring (if it's a mason jar) or a rubber band. The buds are going to swell and excrete water, and this will evaporate out of the top. To protect surfaces, you should place the jar on a plate to catch overflow. Replace the paper towel as needed.

4. Stir the mixture daily for at least four weeks. Make sure the buds stay submerged or they will likely mold. It's okay if they're floating—they will sink eventually—if they're submerged in the oil.

5. The oil should be ready in about six weeks but can safely brew for up to a year. It will be fine to use if there's no mold and the jar is kept covered and buds submerged. When you're ready, strain off the oil and store in a labeled and dated bottle in a cool dry place. Be sure to mark somewhere on the bottle or jar that it's for magical use only and not for consumption!

We all have loving and supportive ancestors. Research and reach out. We can draw upon these ancestral relationships for insight, to increase our health and well-being, and for support in our day-to-day life.

14

Crystals for Genealogy Magic

Crystals are living beings at the beginning of creation.

—Nikola Tesla

Crystals are a popular way to add magic, beauty, and power to everyday life, and especially to your genealogy magic! They're typically portable, extremely versatile, and come in a wide range of colors and correspondences. I consider them an important tool for my genealogy work. I generally use crystals as part of a sacred grid on my altar, and I carry one or more with me in a purse or pocket, or in the form of jewelry. Creating a crystal grid is an especially beautiful and meaningful way to focus your intention on a particular person, place, or to accomplish a goal. There are many ways to create a crystal grid and you should always do what works best for you.

For the center of the grid, I use a flat palm stone. This is the base of all the work I do, and it's infused with my intention to be successful in my research. I suggest getting one that is flat and level when it's laid down so that other smaller items, like a picture, or another crystal, can be placed on top as needed. If you're not planning to set anything on top of the center stone, a cabochon is also something to consider. They often come in different shapes—oval, round, heart, diamond—so choose one that resonates for you.

It's important to cleanse your crystals before using them for any genealogy work. I like to do this by placing them under the light of a full moon.

There are other ways you can cleanse your crystals: sacred smoke, a sound bath from a bell or a singing bowl, sunlight, or sprinkled with a blessing water of your own creation. If you use water, be sure to wipe it off right away as some crystals don't do well when they get wet and remain that way.

The space where you will be putting your crystal grid should also be prepared. Clear and wipe down the surface. Consider using a base to designate the sacred space. This base can be made from a grid drawn on paper, a grid printed on cloth, or a carved wooden grid base. When I am preparing my space, I clear the energy with my rosemary clearing spray, and I light my orange seven-day candle. Music is also a great way to add a certain a certain kind of energy to the space.

Next, decide what your intentions are for the grid. Do you want to locate records for a certain ancestor? For example, "I want to find more information on _____ (ancestor's name)." Write your intention down on a piece of paper and place it, along with a picture if you have one, in the center of your grid. It's best to be specific, however, you can also create a general purpose grid to support your intention of continued success in your genealogy work.

Consider the energy you need this grid to manifest for you. Consider the individual properties of certain crystals but also think about simply being intuitive and choosing the grid's crystals that way. Most grids are constructed from the center outward, but I have done spirals to send energy out or in, as was needed. You can also consider if you want to work with a certain element and choose crystals that reflect that energy. For example, when I am working with my mother line, I lean toward fiery crystals like carnelian, as I associate fire with my maternal lineage.

Once you've written your intention for the grid, place the paper in the center of your space. Hold the center stone in your dominant hand and state your intention for the grid out loud. Top it with the clear quartz palm stone (or whatever you've chosen). Begin to surround the center stone with other objects. I like to be very symmetrical with my placements. I also use flowers, stems of rosemary, pebbles I've collected, and other objects that symbolize something in particular to me. This is a chance to really stretch your intuitive muscles and consider deeply how different objects resonate for you. There is no right or wrong, go with what feels best for you.

After your grid is set up, you will need to activate it. I have a small clear quartz wand that I use just for activating grids. You can also use your own finger if you feel comfortable doing that. This activation is an energetic connecting of the crystals, so take your time and mentally draw a line between each one so that the entirety of the grid is linked. You can sing, hum, or speak your intention again as you activate. Once it's activated, just let it do its work. I like to leave mine up for at least twenty-four hours, but usually longer. I find most of mine are taken down around the three-day mark, but feel free to leave yours in place for as long as the crystals stay in position and there is no wilting of any flowers or stems that are part of its construction.

When you disassemble your crystal grid, work from the outside in. As you remove the crystals, thank them for their energetic addition to your magic. Set them aside for cleansing. Burn the petition paper in a safe place and put plant material outdoors to decompose naturally.

Here I share my favorite crystals, along with a few suggestions on how you can utilize each one. Remember that you create your own magic, however, so if one or more of these doesn't resonate with you, or if you want to use them differently, please do so. For example, sometimes I will use a crystal simply because I want the energy of its color.

The magic you create is the most powerful.

Amethyst is a gorgeous purple quartz crystal that ranges in color from soothing light lavender to dazzling deep violet. It is a go-to crystal for many practitioners because of its versatility, effectiveness, and ease of use. Amethyst is said to enhance spiritual connection and psychic ability, provide protection, promote focus and clarity. It also acts as a karmic healer, which is helpful when dealing with those recent ancestors with whom we shared some pain in the past. Overall, it's a must-have in your genealogy magic toolbox.

Suggestions:

- Use a piece of amethyst to represent the element of spirit in rituals, spells, and other magical workings.

- Hold a piece of amethyst in your hand and infuse it with your desire to connect to a certain ancestor, then place it next to your Mirror of Connection to increase the back-and-forth energy flow, and for protection.

- Keep amethyst on your desk or wherever you do your genealogy research to support a clear mind and concentration, and to increase intuition when researching.

- Wear amethyst jewelry. This allows you to be hands-free while engaging in creative pursuits like genealogy-inspired painting or writing, and who doesn't look good in purple? It's higher vibration with style!

- Carry amethyst for protection and shielding when you're away from home, especially if you like to engage in genealogy hobbies like wandering cemeteries. Jewelry works well for this.

Blue Lace Agate is a beautiful pale blue crystal with white streaks, thought to facilitate peace of mind and the speaking of personal truths. It is also believed to neutralize anger and dissolve old patterns. These qualities are excellent for those seeking family truths who may have been rejected or to whom lies have been told. It also aids in the accurate retelling of genealogical family stories while journaling, and the creation of new ones that reflect the family of influence or choice.

Suggestions:

- Use a piece of blue lace agate to represent the element of water in rituals, spells, and other magical workings.

- Carry blue lace agate to family gatherings where tension might be high, and you need to keep peace of mind. A small piece in a pocket can serve as a touchstone, or wear a piece of jewelry, such as a pendant, so the stone is easily in reach.

- When journaling about genealogical family stories, set a piece of blue lace agate on the edge of your paper or near your keyboard to ensure accuracy and detail, and to unblock personal truths.

- To facilitate the creation or retelling of a story about your family of influence or choice, place a blue candle near your workspace, light it, and set a piece of blue lace agate near it.

- Before reaching out to DNA matches, especially if you are searching for clues to solve a mystery, create a small altar with a blue candle surrounded by three blue lace agate stones alternating with three double-terminated clear quartz points. Light the candle as needed. Envision peace and honest words in all interactions. This will help to keep the mind at ease while encouraging the other party to share their truths.

Bloodstone, also known as heliotrope, is a potent crystal comprised of dark green jasper and small inflections of iron oxide. The spots of red can resemble drops of blood, hence the name. Bloodstone has many functions, but its reputation as an energy cleanser and blood purifier are two properties that make it an excellent tool for genealogy. As a stone of courage, it is useful for all works geared toward making connections to genealogical family, and genealogy research. It aids with dreams and the exploration of past lives, both of which can provide insight to current issues surrounding family dynamics.

Suggestions:

- To encourage dreams that offer an increased perception of family matters, past and present, hold the bloodstone in your hand and speak your intent, then place it under your pillow. In the morning, be sure to journal your dreams. Cleanse the bloodstone under running water or place it in a sunny windowsill.

- Use one or more bloodstones on an altar or in a sacred circle to represent yourself or your genealogical ancestors, or both.

- Create a bloodstone-infused oil and anoint candles to burn while you do the work of discovering where DNA matches fit in your family tree.

- For courage, place a bloodstone next to your computer while researching ancestors that may have engaged in unsavory or illegal actions.

Citrine is a beautiful, sunny crystal with color variations that span the yellow-orange spectrum. Derived from the French word citron, or lemon, citrine has a protective energy that drives away negativity, both in verbal and written form. In its darker shades, citrine is good to have on hand when dealing with the spiritual aspects of genealogy and research, especially if the interactions or experiences could be less than positive. Citrine absorbs negative energy, transmutes it, and expels it, either by sending it to ground or out into the universe. In another of its aspects, citrine is also good for attracting abundance and prosperity, and enhancing psychic connections. I use it when working on brick walls, or blocks, to attract what is needed for my research. If you're searching for information on a reclusive ancestor, citrine can help by bringing a wealth of information your way.

*Be aware that some citrine is heat-treated amethyst.

Suggestions:

- Use a piece of citrine to represent the element of fire in rituals, spells, and other magical workings.

- Keep a citrine point in the upright position near your research area to absorb, transmute, and move negative energy up and away from the space.

- When working on difficult research problems, charge a small piece of citrine by holding it in your hand, envision your desired goal, then place it next to a lighted yellow candle.

- Wear citrine against your skin to help keep your thoughts clear and prevent distraction while researching.

- If you engage in sessions of automatic writing, place a piece of citrine near the paper to activate genetic memories and increase psychic power.

Clear Quartz is a clear white, or colorless, stone called krystallos by the Greek, meaning ice. Much like a white candle, clear quartz stands on its own, with its own qualities, and stands in place of others when needed. It is an illuminator, shining light on the unknown. It is an amplifier that powers up any magical working in which it is included. It is known by some as a "cosmic computer" and holds information. If I had to pick only a few crystals to use in my genealogy work, clear quartz would be in my top two (the other being obsidian), and I'd have it in the form of a palm stone.

Suggestions:

- Keep a "record keeper" clear quartz on your workspace to help connect you to ancestral lines and to amplify your access to information while researching.

- Use double-terminated clear quartz points in grids, mandalas, on your altar, desk, or both. Anywhere you need to push and pull energy or intent in and out of a space. To send energy or intent in one direction, use a single-terminated clear quartz point.

- Carry a clear quartz in your purse or pocket when you go to research repositories, like a library or records archive. This will help to amplify your connection to ancestral documents.

Hematite has a metallic luster and ranges in color from black to silver to reddish-brown. It contains a high amount of iron and is therefore closely associated with blood. It is a stone of intense detox-ification and can help to remove toxic feelings that have built up over long periods of time. Letting go of this toxicity is an essential part of ancestral healing, especially regarding the relatives with whom we have contact. Hematite is also protective and very grounding.

Suggestions:

- Keep a large piece of hematite nearby during intense work that involves toxic relationships and healing them.

- Wear a piece of hematite jewelry when you will physically be around toxic family. This will help to protect you, keep you grounded, and allow negative feelings to simply roll away.

- Anoint black candles with a hematite-infused oil and light these candles whenever you feel that you need to process and do the work of letting go of toxic blockages that are keeping you from being emotionally whole.

Kunzite varies in color from soft pink to pale purple and is named after the mineralogist George Kunz, who first described its appearance. Kunzite carries an essence of love within it, and it has a direct connection to the heart and crown chakras. It carries a peaceful energy to it that makes it very useful for use in scenarios of heartbreak or endings that can cause a bit of regret or sadness, as it is believed to ease heartache and calm nerves.

Suggestions:

- Use kunzite in rituals of ending to promote a peaceful heart and a calm atmosphere.

- Wear kunzite jewelry to memorial services and funerals to help with the easing of heartache.

- Keep kunzite on the altar near pictures or written names of deceased loved ones when energetic assistance is needed to promote a peaceful and loving spiritual relationship, especially if things were contentious while the person was living.

Lapis Lazuli is a visually stunning crystal in varying shades of brilliant blue. Inclusions of white calcite and pyrite give it distinctive streaks of white and yellow. It is a stone of reflection that can help you to confront certain truths and gain a clearer perspective. It amplifies psychic potential and enhances the ability to receive imagery and other guidance during divinatory work with ancestors and ancestral energies, and it assists with dream remembrance. Lapis lazuli is reminiscent of the night sky in its appearance and can help you feel a cosmic-level connection to your ancestry.

Suggestions:

- Use a piece of lapis lazuli to represent the element of air in rituals, spells, and other magical workings.

- Keep lapis lazuli under your pillow, or near your sleeping space, to help you recall dreams. Be sure to journal about your dreams immediately upon wakening.

- To enhance connections and increase receptivity and clarity, anoint a candle with lapis lazuli-infused oil, then light it prior to meditation or divinatory work.

- Carry a piece of lapis lazuli in your pocket or purse when visiting cemeteries where ancestors are interred. Keep your mind open to receive images or sounds during your visit.

- Wear lapis lazuli close to the skin to amplify your psychic ability in regard to your genealogy research, to increase your success in finding records, or to enhance the connections you feel with certain ancestors.

Moonstone is an opalescent stone that can be found in many colors including peach, pink, gray, green, blue, yellow, and brown. It's part of the mineral family of feldspars. It's well-known for its connection to the sacred feminine, it increases intuition, and provides balance. It is a popular crystal for women and is used for protection in travel and childbirth. It calms and releases stress. Moonstone is, of course, also associated with the Moon.

Suggestions:

- Use a piece of moonstone to represent the sacred feminine in rituals, spells, and other magical workings.

- Wear moonstone jewelry when gathered with other women of the family to increase the combined power of the sacred feminine and to promote positive bonding.

Obsidian most often occurs in shades of black and deep brown. This is an extremely powerful stone of protection, truth, and integrity, and is one of the top two I'd choose (the other being clear quartz) if I had to limit the number of crystals I keep. Obsidian is a strong shielding stone, it protects the aura from negativity and harm, and cleanses away energetic debris and blockages from the past while simultaneously serving as a means of grounding and promoting clarity.

Suggestions:

- Keep obsidian near the workspace to protect the aura from email or chat communications that may be unpleasant or sent with the intent to cause emotional distress.

- During ritual work that involves calling in ancestors or ancestral energies, place obsidian near a lit black candle and consciously invoke its protective energy.

- Hold a piece of snowflake obsidian in the dominant hand while meditating on complicated issues such as ancestral healing to provide protection and shielding, cleansing away of mental blocks, and to offer grounding and clarity.

- Wear a piece of obsidian jewelry to any family gathering in which there will likely be a manifestation of dysfunction. Touch it often to ground and shield.

Petrified (Fossilized) Wood is the name given to fossilized remains of woody plants that have been long buried in wet sediments containing dissolved minerals. It is said to connect to the Akashic Records, enabling one to connect to past lives. It represents our ancient ancestry, and that energy can assist you with making a connection to yourself at the cellular level, thus accessing knowledge stored within your DNA, commonly referred to as "genetic memory." It also can help with increasing patience, which is a necessary virtue when doing genealogy work! Some pieces of petrified wood have rings and connecting with a specific ring can lead you to information about a specific past life.

Suggestions:

- Use a piece of petrified wood to represent the element of earth in rituals, spells, and other magical workings.

- During periods of research in which you find yourself short of patience, hold a piece of petrified wood in your dominant hand and envision the energies of the deep past washing through you, giving you the ease you need to continue working productively.

- Meditate with a piece of petrified wood that has visible rings. You will be guided to a specific ring. Ask to be given information about the past life connected with that ring. Place the petrified wood under your pillow when you go to sleep to dream of past lives. Upon awakening, journal the details of any dreams you remember.

- Keep petrified wood on your altar or workspace, or both when engaging in work that revolves around ancestral healing. This will help you connect at the cellular level to bring forth genetic memories to begin the healing process. (Reminder: Some people need therapy support during healing work, please check in with your medical provider.)

Rose Quartz is a popular crystal that comes in a range of delightful shades, from a nearly white blush pink to a deep rosy hot pink. It is a stone of love, inviting in the energy of that steady kind of commitment that one sees with established couples and other healthy relationships. It evokes a sense of calm and works well to reduce anxiety when dealing with stressful issues surrounding DNA testing results, research, and contact of matches. It represents the heart in all types of magical work.

Suggestions:

- Use a rose quartz palm stone in the center of a mandala to represent the steady love of family (even if it's not your current reality). Use double-terminated clear quartz points around the rose quartz to increase the loving energy.

- Wear a piece of rose quartz jewelry to family gatherings to encourage a peaceful and loving atmosphere.

- Carry a piece of rose quartz in your pocket or purse and use it as a touchstone to remind you to keep your boundaries strong and to protect your heart against hurt.

- Add a chip of rose quartz to an essential oil roller with a scented oil of your choice. Apply to inner wrist points to encourage a calm demeanor and remind you that you are worthy of love.

Tiger's Eye is a variety of quartz that displays a quality known as chatoyancy, which makes it resemble the eye of a tiger or a cat. It is opaque and its color ranges from golden to brown red, usually with black stripes, and it looks silky. Sometimes it is dyed. It is associated with the divine masculine and is known as a stone of courage and good luck. It is protective and shields against draining energies.

Suggestions:

- Use a piece of tiger's eye to represent the divine masculine in rituals, spells, and other magical workings.

- When you need to summon a courageous energy to manage certain situations, hold a piece of tiger's eye in your dominant hand and say to yourself, "I am filled with courage." Carry it with you while you complete your encounter.

- Wear tiger's eye jewelry to any situation, whether in-person or through tech like Zoom or phone, to manifest strength and to keep draining energies outside your bubble.

15

Notable Ancestors

GiGi, do we have pirates in our family tree?
Because I really want there to be pirates.

—Silas, age seven

One of the most popular genealogy activities is searching for famous, or infamous, ancestors. I have distant cousins in Australia who are very proud of their "convict" ancestors. Many people look for royalty within their tree's branches. Men are often thrilled to find out their Y-DNA can be attributed to Irish High King Niall of the Nine Hostages. People with mitochondrial haplogroup K might be delighted to know that Mary Magdalene is purported to be part of that mother line. Others are excited to discover the accomplishments of an ancestor, especially when done so despite challenging life circumstances.

I discovered that I am a direct descendant of the Philip Salladay family of Ohio. They got caught up in the New England vampire panic back in 1816 to 1817, which was actually fueled by a tuberculosis outbreak. They believed the wasting respiratory illness continued to infect family members because the deceased walked among the family at night while they were asleep. A decision was made to disinter the most recently deceased, Philip's son Samuel, cut away his internal organs, then burn them while surviving family inhaled the smoke. It's a frightful scene, really, but I find it intriguing as a medical person how generations past tried to make sense of, and cure, diseases before the advent of modern day science. Unfortunately, their gruesome cure did not work as intended and the entire Salladay family succumbed to tuberculosis, save one son, George, from whom I descend (along with his wife Phoebe Chaffin Salladay). It's always interesting to find ancestors that are noteworthy for one reason or another. Thankfully I have other, more palatable, stories that are included in my notable ancestor file!

Witches

Searching for witches in the family tree is very popular for many magical people of European descent who walk a genealogy path, and in fact is the most common request I hear from those who are searching for notable people in their tree! It's helpful when searching to know some of the history that prompted the labeling of certain people as a witch. I feel like some people take a whimsical approach to having an ancestor connected to the accusation of witchcraft, however, the reality of those times is rife with negativity that left a lasting mark on the generations that followed.

The witch hunter's manual Malleus Malificarum—typically translated from the Latin as the "Hammer of Witches"—was published in 1486, but condemnation of malefecium (literally "bad-doing" but often indicating "witchcraft") and sortilegium (fortune-telling) in Europe began several hundred years earlier, around 910, although there were also arguments during this era that many stories of those acts were not based in reality. Unfortunately, the paranoia surrounding witchcraft had increased significantly by the time the Malleus was published, which then only served to increase the panic. Within its pages are suggestions for how to perform torture to obtain confessions and it states that the death penalty, often done in such a way as to inflict the most pain and misery, was the only way to contain the evils of witchcraft. The book influenced culture and was essentially a guidebook for hunting, torturing, and killing people, especially women, under the guise of eradicating witchcraft.

With the exception of very few regions, the majority of those accused of witchcraft during the witch panic in Christian Europe and its colonies were usually women who were marginalized in some way and preyed upon by men who wished to seize, or feel, power. Men were also accused, convicted, and executed, but it is estimated that between 75 to 80 percent of those executed for witchcraft were women. Accusations of witchcraft were often hurled as a means of revenge, or to keep the accuser from being accused. These "witches"—often healers, or those who subscribed to local folkloric customs and beliefs of the time—suffered greatly at the hands of those who sought to persecute and torture them prior to sentencing them to a horrific death.

By the 1500s, the paranoia surrounding witches and the resultant witch hunting craze was just getting into full swing. While the number of trials and executions varies, it is generally thought that approximately 110,000 persons in total have been tried for witchcraft, and between forty thousand to sixty thousand have been executed. As of this writing, the most recent known execution of a person for witchcraft was in Somalia, in 2020. Sadly, the misconceptions and persecution continue.

Other Notable Ancestors of Interest

After witches, there are several categories of ancestors that people seem particularly thrilled to find within their lineage tree, even if it's simply the association of descending from a sibling or cousin, or even a family connection to the same town, social circle, or time period. Royalty tops the list, as do presidents and other world leaders, politicians, celebrities, literary persons, suffragettes, activists, survivors, world explorers, those who've fled religious and political persecution, pirates, and vampires, and, in the United States, the backbone of three major lineage societies, American Revolutionary War soldiers (Daughters of the American Revolution and Sons of the American Revolution) and Mayflower passengers (Mayflower Society).

Consider your own ancestors, and how they manifest themselves in your life today. Perhaps you are descended from a farmer, and you have a love of the land and a talent for making things grow. There might be a seamstress or tailor in your past who was gifted at piecing together bits of fabric into beautiful, or functional, clothing for the family, and you have a penchant for textiles too. Are you a wordsmith with an author in your lineage? An artist descended from an artist? We often find hints of ourselves in the past, if we take the time to look for them and learn about our ancestors.

Research

There are countless ways to research for the many kinds of notable ancestors, but first you must define what that ancestor might look like for you. For me, notable includes someone who is somehow marked out in history for an unusual occurrence, like my "vampire" ancestors. It also includes an ancestor with whom I feel a connection, like I do with my grandmother and great-aunts who read cards (among other things). For others, the notability of an ancestor might come from them occupying a shining place in the annals of time, a person who is well-known and remembered, like royalty, or a celebrity. For still others, finding the name of an ancestor who simply survived, and thrived, makes them notable. All scenarios are valid and none too frivolous to merit research and the joy of discovery.

As you search for notable folk in your lineage, pay attention to surnames. I have a list of all surnames in my tree; this can usually be compiled by family tree software or by hand. You won't necessarily know that an ancestor is someone that you might consider to be notable. I had no idea that my Salladay ancestors were quite so interesting until I'd exchanged emails with a distant cousin who sent me a link to a story about their graveside ritual. When you do recognize a potential notable ancestor, be sure to utilize the internet. One easy way I do an initial search is to place their name in quotes and then add "genealogy" behind it, perhaps along with a year. Many online resources list names and dates and give other details about the person. Some sites will have specific lists regarding a collective population, like witches. Helpful information for genealogists will sometimes be included, like names of spouse and children. Some surnames have societies for descendants and those invariably will have at least one avid researcher as a member.

Other surnames are notable on their own, even if just for their meaning. I am a fourth great-granddaughter of Mary Nankivell Lathlean of St. Agnes, Cornwall who, after her husband Lancelot Lathlean was killed in a mining accident in 1840, ventured by ship across the Atlantic Ocean with only her children and settled in Schuylkill County, Pennsylvania. The surname Nankivell has deep roots in Cornwall, with its earliest recording dated around 1324. While researching this intriguing surname, I came across various bits of research about its old Cornish family. I first read that the origin of the name Nankivell was said to derive from nan/nant/nance, which is Cornish for "valley" and the personal name of Cyfel, or perhaps the Welsh Ceffyl, meaning "horses." This is thought to be inaccurate by a researcher named Edmund Typpett Nankivell, who refers to the book, "The Registers of St Columb Major, Cornwall—1539 to 1780" published in 1881. It says, "The name Nankivell is pure Keltic, and means "Glen of the Woodcocks"; a glen so-called (generally spelt Nanskevall), with its old oak wood, lies about two miles from St. Columb." The Nanskeval Cottage remains intact on the private lands of Carnaton House Estate. There is a foot path that passes near the rear of the cottage, and the Nanskeval Farm is mentioned in Direction #33 of the walk, which states:

> *Cross the stile and bear left onto the track. Follow it until it ends at a gate and stile before lane. In 1819, an ingot of tin weighing nearly 18kg was found at Nanskeval Farm, buried nearly a metre below the surface in swampy ground. It was cast in Roman times, probably using an open granite mould, and is stamped with the head of a soldier wearing a Roman helmet. It is now in the Truro Museum.*

I use my own Nankivell surname story here as an example of the information that can be gleaned by simply searching a surname online, or by connecting with others researching the same surname. The Nankivell sur-name might not be very notable to many others, but it's notable to me that I descend from people who hail from, and called themselves after, a glen of woodcocks, who built a farm and cottage on land once occupied by Roman soldiers, and who have a long history in a beautiful land that I love so very much.

One of the best ways to link yourself to any person from the past is to build out a solid tree of your own, including shrubbing (see chapter 5—Three Trees), back to the time frame in which you are looking to connect. This is how I am able to connect to so many interesting tidbits within my own tree. Every time you add a grandmother to a tree, you add a new family surname that opens a door to more history, more stories. Building out a tree is time-consuming, but worth the effort, even if it means you only possess a tree that is flush with information!

Regarding my own tree, and the quest to know if I have witch ancestors, I have yet to find a direct connection to any witches of the past. However, I do have same-surname ancestors in Massachusetts around the time of the Salem witch trials. I think sometimes on the anxiety that must've been felt by so many people who worried that they might be next. That's something to consider when working on your genealogy and considering how collec-tive trauma and dysfunction have impacted your genetic memory carried in your energetic DNA. People traveled to escape religious persecution, and I believe that accusations of witchcraft, or fear of that, were surely a part of some ancestral migrations.

While you might not be descended directly from a notable person, you can look for similar surnames that also come from the same village, town, or city. Remember that populations were a lot smaller back then, so people with the same surname were often related in some way, either by blood or marriage. Consider social circles, churches, and other scenarios in which people connected as a source of information as well. Look for books that talk about the history of a location. There will likely be surnames of found-ing residents included. Remember to make a research plan and document your journey to discover these potential ancestors just like you would with any other genealogy project or goal.

Journal Magic

Light your orange candle and open your Mirror of Connection to let the energy of the past flow through to you. Place a piece of citrine near the candle. Think about your own innate talents and strengths. Say aloud:

Beloved ancestors, think now on your earthly accomplishments, both large and small. Please share them with me now so that I may celebrate you with pride!

Write in your journal whatever comes to mind, or draw, even if it doesn't make much sense. When you are done, snuff the candle and be sure to firmly close the Mirror and cover it. Sleep with the citrine under your pillow, or on your nightstand, and journal again in the morning about any dreams you remember.

Consider one bit of information as the most important about your ancestors: they survived, at least long enough to create the next generation. I strive daily to discover as many of mine as I can, to speak their names, to elevate them in my own way. I think very highly of all the "common people" within my tree who are not famous within the annals of history but who are precious to me in all their worldly anonymity, because I would not exist without them. For me, that is the most notable fact of all.

16

Remembrance

Remember me in the family tree; my name, my days, my strife.
Then I'll ride upon the wings of time and live an endless life.

—Linda Goetsch

Working with ancestors is a central fixture in most magical practices. Those from whom we descend come from many places and all walks of life, and, while we can never know them all, we can certainly research and enlarge and enrich our Tree of Lineage with as much detail as we can find. Reaching into the past allows us to find a beautiful and meaningful connection to our roots and our heritage.

There are many ways to connect with the ancestors. Two of my favorite ways are the ancestor altar, and a garden or green space dedicated to the ancestors.

Building an Ancestor Altar

Earlier in the book, I mentioned the importance of creating a sacred space in which to do genealogy work. One way to manifest a sacred space for genealogy work is to build an ancestor altar. There is no one right way to do this, as it depends on personal preference and aesthetic. Altars are very individual. Some people prefer a simpler space—perhaps a small table with a plain cloth and a candle. Others use an outdoor space. I've seen altars to water goddesses in bathrooms and kitchens. When it's an option, space-wise, I prefer an elaborate altar filled with all manner of items that represent the people, places, and things that are important to me. Every kind of altar is exactly what is needed for the person who creates it.

For those who want to create a sacred space for honoring the ancestors and don't know where to start, the first step is to look within. What's your preferred aesthetic? What can you afford? What other aspects of your lifestyle will affect the space? Small children, pets (especially cats, curious animals possessing the capacity to jump and access spaces other pets cannot), and inquisitive visitors or roommates can all have an impact on where you decide to set up this altar. For those who require it, one clever option is to create an ancestor altar that hides in plain sight.

Once you've chosen the best location and aesthetic, you are ready to get started.

Items for Your Ancestor Altar

Define the space. Use a table covering or a piece of cloth to serve as a base of some sort, in a color that appeals to you. For an ancestor altar, I like white or red. I also like cloths with fringe and patterns. Others prefer the simplicity and clean look of a simple cloth.

Having a heat-safe dish or plate on which to place candles so they can burn safely is a necessity. There are many options: a plate or platter, a small cauldron filled with sand, or an heirloom dish that is sturdy enough to be handled regularly.

Framed photographs of family and other ancestors of influence are a wonderful tool for cultivating a relationship.

Candles are a lovely way to bring warmth and intention to the ancestral altar space. The type of candle is a personal choice, as long as it will light and keep burning. I have used all kinds of candles—tapers, small chime or spell candles, five- and seven-day candles, and tea lights. The candle color is also up to you. For my ancestor altar, I prefer a white candle unless I'm doing specific work for which I would prefer another color. For example, I like to use green when doing health-related petitions or to ask for assistance with researching the family tree.

Make regular offerings of food and drink to your ancestors as a way to honor them, especially if you've been doing other, specific, work with them.

Bring the energy of an ancestor to your sacred space with family heirlooms. The object doesn't have to be anything expensive; it only has to have meaning for you. I have a booklet that my grandmother got from her church right before she died, and its cover image of Our Lady of Prompt Succor reminds me of the sacred feminine. This booklet sits on my altar in a crystal punch bowl that also belonged to her.

Represent the elements of water, earth, fire, and air. I keep a small bowl of water, a vase of fresh flowers and a bit of dirt from various ancestral places I've visited, a seven-day candle burning continuously, and a small feather.

Keep a small, framed mirror to represent the ancestors whose names are unknown. This is different than the Mirror of Connection in that it is specifically closed to energy moving through it. Sometimes I will catch a reflection of my own face in it when I am at the altar and it reminds me that I have a large contingent of unknown ancestors from whom I descend, and whose physical and energetic DNA is carried within me.

Other Considerations for Your Ancestor Altar

Keep it clean. I neaten the space once a week, clear out any offerings, burned down candles, and other items that are no longer required. I do a deep cleaning—wash the altar cloth, dust the surface, wipe down photo frames—once a month.

Make offerings regularly. For my maternal grandmother, coffee and a small piece of brioche are my go-to when I want to leave her something special. Otherwise, a cigarette will find its way to her photo, or a small flower, as she loved to garden. For ancestors I didn't know in person, I often leave a bit of brandy.

Reserve the altar space for the dead. I do not keep pictures that include living people on my altar. I also do not keep photos or items from deceased pets there; I have a separate space for them, but that is a personal preference. I know some people who combine the space for people and pets.

How ancestor altars are arranged is also very personal. I find it easiest and safest to keep my candle in the center. I keep photos of ancestors on either side of the candle, along with family heirlooms or other small items that have meaning for me regarding my ancestors. My altar's aesthetic is based on function—I must be able to do the work with ease—but also on beauty. When building your own altar, consider its function along with its form, and work to manifest that vision.

The Ancestral Garden

Gardening is soothing for me and takes me back to my childhood when I would spend many a day working with my grandmother in her garden. She wasn't much of a vegetable grower, preferring instead to nurture flowers, shrubs, trees, and all manner of aesthetically pleasing plants. Her small house was well-known in the neighborhood as a place of plant-based beauty.

My first step into creating a garden space for sitting with the ancestors was when I got the idea that I would plant a pentagram-shaped herb garden. It didn't go well, and I was left with a pentagram-shaped brick garden filled with dirt and dead plants. I realized I do not have a green thumb and my grandmother's skill at tending all things plant and flower did not get passed along, to the point that my mother regularly rescues house plants from me and has done so for years. It's a family joke that if anyone wants a plant, just wait for me to buy one and then they can rescue it from the jaws of death a week or two later. However, what I did learn with the herb garden fiasco is that I am good at creating aesthetic outdoors space. I simply need to do so with hardy plants that I can more easily manage.

I think of the ancestral garden space as a place to connect. We don't all live on the land of our ancestors, or we have ancestors that come from a variety of places. It's not usually considered best practice to plant things that are not native to the area in which one lives; that lesson was learned by me the hard way. However, by creating a lush green space, I feel more able to connect with the earth, and to manifest an energetic connection with the ancestral energies that surround me. If you have the space, consider giving some of it to growing your own space for ancestral connection. Pick colors and plant types that resonate for you.

In addition to plants, consider adding other items like a bench, or chairs and table, for sitting and communing, small houses for the winged creatures, a water feature that also serves as a drinking station for the wild inhabitants, and some garden sculptures of your own preference. These all add to the ambiance of the space and make it a destination that you will want to visit every day. I also have a small altar set up in my own garden on which I can place magical items that are suited to being out in the elements. I can also do ritual work outside in this space.

If you live in a space that doesn't have much allowance for an outdoor garden, consider a container garden. Also, utilize public green spaces in and around your home. Connections can be made with the ancestors of place in the spaces to which we have traveled, too. Simply have a seat and close your eyes!

The "Mary Unknowns"

Names are important. Whether we use the one given to us, or the one we choose for ourselves, it's most meaningful when our name is used in any scenario, other than one that calls for anonymity. In too much historical documentation, women are often referred to only in reference to their status as daughter, wife, or mother. The first or nickname is sometimes accompanied by the husband's surname. The family surname—or maiden name—seems to disappear often as women moved from daughter to wife. Women are also referred to by Mrs. and then their husband's name will follow. Overall, the loss of women's family surnames in the historical record had led to many brick walls that cannot be knocked down. It also speaks volumes as to the lack of importance of and regard for women's roles, and their meaning in societies of the recent genealogical past.

Originally coined by genealogist Lucy Whitfield, the phrase "Mary Unknowns" refers to the women in a family tree who are only known by their first name, nickname, or no name at all. They are near to infinite in number and can present a significant hindrance in bringing a tree to its fullness. Each woman with a missing family surname represents a lineage that cannot be accurately documented, ancestral wisdom that cannot be clearly accessed, and the missed opportunity to create an energetic connection with that grandmother specifically by name.

I have seen so many ways in which people attempt to document the Marys and give them an identifier for their missing family surname. Some use "Unknown." Others use LNU (last name unknown), some use the woman's married surname (please never do that). My least favorite is "None" because that's blatantly inaccurate. The Mary has a family surname, it's just not documented. In my own tree, I refer to the

Mary Unknowns as <First Name> Grandmother. For example, I know that my great-great-great-grandfather's mother was named Elizabeth, but I have yet to find a solid source of documentation that tells me her pre-marriage family surname. I have her in my tree as Elizabeth (first name) Grandmother (last name). It's disconcerting to see a person in documents with no family surname listed, especially in a culture that has them, but I also know realistically we cannot know the full name of every single person from whom we descend. However, in the most recent few hundred years, if the man's name can be known, so should the woman's name. Sadly, that is not the case, however. I encourage anyone engaging in genealogical research to put in the work of discovering the family surnames of their own Mary Unknowns. Success will not always be at hand, but the effort is there. I believe that makes a difference in how we energetically connect to our own Mary Unknowns, even if we never consciously discover them in their fullness.

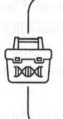

When working on difficult research problems that involve female ancestors, especially those with an unknown family surname, charge a small piece of moonstone by holding it in your hand, envision your desired goal, then place it next to a lighted yellow candle.

Cemeteries and Graveyards

Walking through cemeteries and graveyards wherever I go has been a passion of mine for many years. Spending time with ancestral family is very special, and I find the energy calming and serene. In addition to visiting relatives who are local to me, I also make it a point to seek out those who have been laid to rest in lands far from mine. One of my fondest cemetery memories is coming across the headstone of my 5x g-grandfather in a small cemetery in Cornwall. I felt like I'd stepped back into the past for a moment and made a connection.

There is a certain etiquette that should be maintained when visiting the beloved dead in their resting place. Practices vary and you should do what works best for you, if it is based in respect. Before I enter a cemetery, I stop briefly and mentally knock at the gate to announce my arrival. I ask if my deceased are open to visitation. When I get the affirmative, I enter quietly, leaving a small offering at the gate as thanks to all the inhabitants. My grandmother always left a dime. I will sometimes do that, depending on the structure of the gate or entry. Other times I drop a small flower or other decomposable item that won't interfere with wildlife or cause a mess for the caretaker or groundskeeper. While walking through to your destination grave, be mindful of your noise. If you have children with you, encourage them to be respectful. Animals should be on a leash and any mess picked up and disposed of in an appropriate receptacle.

Visiting the beloved dead at their site of burial is a beautiful way to remember them. On All Saint's Day in New Orleans, families will often have picnics in the cemetery. The tomb is decorated with flowers and other small trinkets, and it is generally an uplifting experience to share a day between the living and the dead.

Some magical people like to do group spells or ritual in the cemetery. I'm of mixed feelings on that, as I have found it disturbing to come across a group of people involved in a loud ritual in the middle of what should be a quiet and reflective space. I tend to think it's not the best place for group rituals. On the other hand, individual work at the site of an ancestor's resting place can be a meaningful way to connect and pay homage to them. Respect and consideration of the beloved dead should always take precedence.

Offerings in remembrance of the beloved dead are always appreciated. Flowers, food, drink (liquor in particular), and money (shiny is best) are the four most popular items left at the grave. Be sure to consider the wildlife before leaving food and be considerate of the people who maintain the grounds. Keep in mind too that quantity is not better than quality when it comes to offerings.

I do need to mention here that you need to be very mindful about what you take from the cemetery. It is not acceptable to remove pieces of any headstone or grave site, and it is against the law to remove bones (and yes, people do that, sadly). Findings on the ground are generally okay as long as they aren't something that could be needed for a repair. These are some things that I've taken from various cemeteries where ancestors are buried: a tiny amount of dirt from a grave site, and only after asking the deceased for permission, small flowers, pinecones, stones that are not part of a grave site and, in New Orleans, random tiny pieces of red brick that are laying around and not a part of any structure that needs repair and . . . pictures! I take a lot of pictures in the cemetery.

It is always good practice to take on the cleaning responsibility for as many ancestral graves as you can manage. While the cemetery generally employs maintenance to take care of the basics, it's a thoughtful descendant who keeps the headstone clean and brings flowers. You can't tend them all but do what you can to make sure the ones most important to you stay well-cared for and clean.

Another consideration, especially for those who prefer to work electronically, is to keep an online space for one or more ancestors. I've seen websites dedicated to distant ancestors that go into detail about their lives and accomplishments. I've seen others that are focused on a close relative who's died recently. One way I've memorialized some of my ancestors is by creating an online memorial on Find a Grave *(www.findagrave.com)*. After making sure there isn't already a memorial in place, I make one and add the details of my ancestor, including pictures. People, including me, can stop by and leave notes and electronic flowers. Attachments can be made from one ancestor to another, creating a repository of familial connections that are great for research (but always confirm these connections with other sources). If you want to create a memorial for an ancestor but find one is already in place, you can request that its management be transferred to you.

Keep in mind, however, that the person who created the memorial may also be a descendant of the deceased. If that's the case, check the entry to make sure it's correct (and if it's not, send a suggestion for corrections), then leave a note and flower.

There are many other ways to remember the beloved dead. One friend of mine has quilts on display that were made by her great-grandmother and an aunt, and she facilitates a cross-cultural quilt block exchange between Irish and American quilters. Another donates money regularly to an animal shelter at which her mother volunteered. It is never a bad thing to do something good in memory of someone. Plant a tree, buy school supplies for a needy child, feed a family for a holiday, sponsor genealogy research for a descendant of an enslaved person . . . the possibilities are nearly endless.

Your Genealogy Legacy Plans

One important aspect of remembrance to consider is your own, and I want to touch very briefly on a topic that can be upsetting to some: end of life planning. In addition to the usual plans that should be in place like an advance directive, a final will and testament, obituary, memorial service, and other instructions for friends and loved ones who will surround you and care for you at the end, you should also have a plan for your genealogy assets.

Genealogist Linda Yip shared this hypothetical scenario on her Past Presence blog:[14]

> *Mary spent 30 years of her life building her family tree and collecting stories, photos, and documents. She travelled to the home country. Her place was a storehouse of family memorabilia. And yet when Mary died, none of her family knew what she owned or knew its value. They cleared her apartment in one weekend by throwing everything out.*

---

[14] Linda Yip Genealogy, Past Presence: *https://past-presence.com*

How does it make you feel to consider that your most important work, art, writing, or other treasures will be tossed out after you die because you don't have a plan for them? The thought of it makes me feel pretty devastated. Most magical people have heard the saying, "What is remembered, lives." One way to ensure this for yourself is to manifest a meaningful legacy plan that ensures your genealogy assets are available for generations to come.

I have been an RN for many years, and I am intimately familiar with the death and dying process . . . for others. Considering the inevitable for myself often brought anxiety and even distress. To help me manage those feelings, I enrolled in a death doula certificate program with the amazing Deathwives at their online Deathschool, and part of their course included legacy work.[15] I've had a plan for my own genealogy assets organized for years, and I was a bit surprised to learn that I still wasn't as prepared as I could've been. I have since reassessed and rewritten my wishes, updated my will, and discussed everything with my family.

What exactly are genealogy assets? It's all the "stuff" you have that relates to genealogy research and documentation, both for yourself and others. Linda Yip describes two kinds: digital and physical.

Digital genealogy assets include:

- Family tree and other work on genealogy websites like FamilySearch, WikiTree, GEDmatch
- Research and other notes on a computer or tablet
- Scanned documents and photos
- Videos and recorded presentations
- DNA test results at websites like Ancestry, 23andMe, MyHeritage, FamilyTreeDNA
- Raw DNA data files downloaded by you onto your computer

Physical genealogy assets include:

- Original paper documents

---

[15] Deathwives: *https://deathwives.org*

- Original photos (please label them all with full names and dates!)
- Books and other published works
- Written and printed materials like your journal, notebooks, research notes, family trees, and family data sheets
- Family mementos that are precious to you

Some questions to ask yourself: What genealogy assets do I have? Who is going to manage them after I'm gone? Where will it all go? How can I make my wishes known? How can I make sure my genealogy assets are available and accessible? If you manage test results or research for others, you should also consider how that will be managed.

Organizing your genealogy assets can be a big job, and it's one you should consider sooner rather than later, especially if it seems overwhelming. Ideally, detailed information about your wishes and the location and disposition of all assets, both physical and digital, should be included in a last will and testament. At minimum, you should ensure that your family or appointed representative can access your genealogy assets by providing a document with usernames and passwords to digital assets, as well as the location of physical assets. Have a conversation with your family or appointed representative and do everything possible to see that your genealogy legacy is handled in the manner most appealing to you.

Finally, what do you want your descendants, and the world, to know about you and your life? Your life story, in your own words, is also a genealogy asset. I always prefer to control my own narrative. If you do too, then take action now. Keep a detailed journal, planner, or both. Create videos in which you share stories about your childhood, your memories, both good and bad, your career, your friends, and your life in general. Continue to research and document your family's genealogy. Make a solid plan for all of your genealogy assets. Your genealogy legacy can be a treasure for the future, but only if you do your best now to make it so.

Conclusion

Genealogy seems to be all the rage these days as people research and do DNA tests to connect with and document the lives and experiences of their ancestors. The option to leave behind a beautiful legacy is available to every person who does the work to make it so. While I find that I am grateful for the joy that genealogy has brought me, there's also been a lot of heartache on my quest for familial truths. I hear the same from others who are also walking the path of the family historian and genealogist. There is a storyteller in each generation of a family who carries the weight of researching and documenting sourced information that will bring the family story forward so that it is accessible for generations to come. It's not always easy, and it's likely that you will shed a few tears of frustration or anger if you take up the mantle of digging into the past to create a family legacy for the future. Surprises and secrets can knock us off balance when they're discovered, and they can tarnish our view of those we love dearly. Living relatives can be uncooperative or dishonest, unsavory ancestors can be revealed, and healing to adjust the family lineage can take many years, or even a lifetime. Along the way, however, there is much happiness, joy, excitement, and a whole lot of magic to be found.

It is my sincere hope that you have found some of that magic within these pages. I wish you well on your genealogy journey!

Resources

Forms for Research and Documentation

An integral part of genealogy research is working within an organized framework. Whenever you sit down to delve into your family tree, be sure to document your work so you don't lose track of your progress. These forms will help you organize your research and keep it in order.

Research Planner & Log

Ancestor:

Research Question:

Date	Repository/Website	Title of Collection	Keyword Search	Results

Family Group Worksheet

Husband/Wife/Partner #1

Full Birth/Chosen Name _____

Birth Date and Place _____

Marriage Date and Place _____

Death Date and Place _____

Burial Date and Place _____

Father/XY/Parent Premarital Name _____

Mother/XX/Parent Premarital Name _____

Husband/Wife/Partner #2

Full Birth/Chosen Name _____

Birth Date and Place _____

Marriage Date and Place _____

Death Date and Place _____

Burial Date and Place _____

Father/XY/Parent Premarital Name _____

Mother/XX/Parent Premarital Name _____

Child's Name and Date/Place of Birth	Partner/Spouse Name & Date/Place of Marriage	Death and Burial Date/Place

Other Information (Previous Marriages, Stepchildren, Etc.)

_____

_____

Ancestor Worksheet

Ancestor Info

Full Premarital Name _____

Birth Date and Place _____

Baptism Date and Place _____

Death Date and Place _____

Burial Date and Place _____

Father's Name _____

Mother's Premarital Name _____

Marriage Date and Place _____

Spouse/Partner Info

Full Premarital Name _____

Birth Date and Place _____

Death Date and Place _____

Burial Date and Place _____

Father's Name _____

Mother's Premarital Name _____

Child's Name and Date/Place of Birth	Partner/Spouse Name & Date/Place of Marriage	Death and Burial Date/Place

Occupation(s) _____

Immigration and Travel (Departure/Arrival Ports, Naturalization Date)
_____
_____

Other Information (Previous Marriages, Stepchildren, Military Service, Education, Etc.)
_____
_____

DNA Match Worksheet

Match's User Name	Testing Company	Shared DNA (% or cM)	Relationship	Most Recent Common Ancestor(s)

DNA Tools, Books, and Blogs

Part of the magic within genealogy are the many tools that are readily available to use and the ease of access to information. Could anyone in the past have ever imagined how we'd be able to communicate so easily via online methods? Or do research from the comfort of our home or office? While research still needs to be done in person for certain records, there are other options for searching and for learning. Here is a short list of my favorite tools, books, blogs, and websites. It is far from comprehensive and likely does not cover all the topics that are of interest and importance to you. Your local library and its staff can be a wonderful free resource, and I encourage you to utilize them and discover your own favorites.

Tools to Use with DNA Testing Results

Instructions for use of the tools are detailed on each website.
DNA Painter Tools: *dnapainter.com*

- Trees
- Chromosome Mapping
- Coverage Estimator
- Shared cM Tool
- What Are The Odds? v1
- Third Party Tools Reference List

GEDMatch: *www.gedmatch.com*
Leeds Method ("DNA Color Clustering: The Leeds Method for Easily Visualizing Matches") *www.danaleeds.com*

Books

Bettinger, Blaine T., *The Family Tree Guide to DNA Testing and Genetic Genealogy, 2nd Edition* (Cincinnati, OH: Family Tree Books, 2019)

Board for Certification of Genealogists, *Genealogy Standards: Second Edition Revised* (Ancestry.com, 2019)

Fessler, Anne, *The Girls Who Went Away: The Hidden History of Women Who Surrendered Children for Adoption in the Decades Before Roe v. Wade* (Penguin Publishing, 2007)

Foor, Daniel, PhD, *Ancestral Medicine: Rituals for Personal and Family Healing* (Bear & Company, 2017)

Hall, Judy, *The Encyclopedia of Crystals, Expanded Edition* (Fair Winds Press, 2013)

Hendrickson, Nancy, *Ancestral Grimoire: Connect with the Wisdom of the Ancestors Through Tarot, Oracles, and Magic* (Weiser Books, 2022)

————, *Unofficial Guide to Ancestry.com: How to Find Your Family History on the #1 Genealogy Website* (F + W Media, 2018)

McCullough, Dana, *Unofficial Guide to FamilySearch.org: How to Find Your Family History on the World's Largest Free Genealogy Website, 2nd Edition* (Cincinnati, OH: Family Tree Books, 2020)

Powell, Kimberly, *The Everything Guide to Online Genealogy: Trace Your Roots, Share Your History, and Create Your Family Tree, 3rd Edition* (Adams Media, 2014)

Smith, Drew, *Organize Your Genealogy: Strategies and Solutions for Every Researcher* (Cincinnati, OH: Family Tree Books, 2016)

Walker, Pete, *Complex PTSD: From Surviving to Thriving: A Guide and Map for Recovering from Childhood Trauma* (CreateSpace Independent Publishing Platform, 2013)

Weinberg, Tamar, *The Adoptee's Guide to DNA Testing: How to Use Genetic Genealogy to Discover Your Long-Lost Family* (Cincinnati, OH: Family Tree Books, 2018)

Wigington, Patti, *Badass Ancestors: Finding Your Power with Ancestral Guides* (Llewellyn Publications, 2020)

Blogs

Ancestry Blog: *https://www.ancestry.com*

Cruwys News: *https://cruwys.blogspot.com*

DNAxPlained—Genetic Genealogy by Roberta Estes: *www.dna-explained.com*

Living DNA: *https://livingdna.com/blog*

Musings on Genealogy, Genetics, and Gardening by Kitty Cooper:
www.blog.kittycooper.com

MyHeritage Blog: *https://blog.myheritage.com*

Six Generations by Stewart Blandón Traiman, MD: *www.sixgen.org*

The DNA Geek by Leah LaPerle Larkin: *www.thednageek.com/blog*

The Enthusiastic Genealogist by Dana Leeds:
www.theenthusiasticgenealogist.blogspot.com

The Legal Genealogist: *https://www.legalgenealogist.com/blog*

The Spittoon: *https://blog.23andme.com*

Through the Trees by Shannon Christmas: *www.throughthetreesblog.tumblr.com*

Your Genetic Genealogist by CeCe Moore: *www.yourgeneticgenealogist.com*

Websites

Adoptee and Misattributed Parentage Resources

The ALMA Society: *https://thealmasociety.org*

American Adoption Congress: *www.americanadoptioncongress.org*

Bastard Nation: *https://bastards.org*

International Soundex Reunion Registry: *www.isrr.org*

Right to Know: *https://righttoknow.us*

Search Angels: *www.searchangels.org*

There are also many state- and local-level organizations that work on behalf of adoptee rights. Search online in your area to access them.

Online Mental Health Resources

Alma Virtual Therapy: *https://helloalma.com*

Anxiety and Depression Association of America: *www.adaa.org*
TalkSpace Anxiety Therapy: *www.talkspace.com*

Family Tree Software
Family Tree Maker: *https://www.mackiev.com*
Gramps: *https://gramps-project.org*
Legacy Family Tree: *https://legacyfamilytree.com*
MyHeritage; "Family Tree Builder": *www.myheritage.com*
RootsMagic (My favorite!): *www.rootsmagic.com*

DNA Testing and Research
23 and Me: *www.23andMe.com*
Ancestry: *www.dna.Ancestry.com*
Family Tree DNA: *www.FamilyTreeDNA.com*
Living DNA: *www.LivingDNA.com*
My Heritage: *www.MyHeritage.com*

Genealogy Research
AfriGeneas: *www.afrigeneas.com*
BillionGraves: *www.billiongraves.com*
Chinese Family History: *https://chinesefamilyhistory.org*
Chronicling America: *www.chroniclingamerica.loc.gov*
Cyndi's List: *www.cyndislist.com*
Family Tree Magazine: "Best European Genealogy Websites"—by David
    Fryxell: *www.familytreemagazine.com*
FamilyTreeMagazine.com (Try the free resources!): *www.familytreemagazine.com*
Find a Grave: *www.findagrave.com*
Find My Past: *https://findmypast.com*
Fold3: *www.fold3.com*
GenealogyBank: *www.genealogybank.com*
Google (including Google Translate and Google Books): *www.google.com*
Haplogroup: *www.haplogroup.org*

Historical Newspapers: *www.newspapers.com*
Irish Genealogy: *www.irishgenealogy.ie*
ISOGG Wiki: *www.isogg.org*
JewishGen: *www.jewishgen.org*
National Indian Law Library: "Tracing Native American Family Roots"
  https://narf.org
New England Historic Genealogical Society's American Ancestors:
  www.americanancestors.org

Genealogical Societies

American Society of Genealogists: *www.fasg.org*
Association of Professional Genealogists: *www.apgen.org*
National Genealogical Society: *www.ngsgenealogy.org*
Rootsweb Wiki List of Genealogical Societies: *https://wiki.rootsweb.com*

Acknowledgments

Without the love and support of my awesome husband, Kirk, this book wouldn't exist. Thank you, my love, for the endless encouragement and for serving as the impetus for me to take up the journey of genetic genealogy. You are my everything. Hot coffee and apple pie fika forever!

My daughters are my most exacting teachers and my heart's joy. My brilliant beauties, I am so proud of the women you've become. I love you both beyond words.

My mother, Susan, experienced the kind of genealogical shock that can shake a person to their core. Mom, I thank you for allowing me to share parts of your difficult story. You are uniquely you, and you were, and are, loved by many. Always keep that in your heart.

My father was an adventurous sort, and I know he would've enjoyed the journey of hunting for his paternal roots. Dad, thank you for showing up in spirit as I did the hard work of healing. I know in my heart and mind that you loved me so much, and I carry that with me. Wherever you are, I pray you have found peace, potato chips, cold beer, and a winning football team.

Ain't no joy like a 9th Ward boy! My grandsons are a most precious gift that have filled my heart with a love I couldn't imagine before their arrival. Sweet boys, my genealogy wish for you is that you will one day look upon your thoroughly researched and well-sourced eight generation tree with excitement and gratitude and that you will remember your ancestors and share them with your own descendants.

Family research is made so much easier with family participation. For all the family and family-in-law that I have subjected to incessant hounding about DNA tests, thank you for spitting and letting me dig through the results. Your contributions have brought healing, connections, and fullness to what was a very sad and battered tree. I am so grateful.

A true "BFF" is a treasure. I am fortunate that mine has been with me for nearly thirty years now, standing by my side in love, laughter, and support through all manner of trials and triumphs. Christine, you are a luminous star that shines so brightly in my little universe. Never change. I love you so much.

It's true that opposites attract. My dear friend, partner, and the other half of my silver wheel, Laura Louella, encouraged me to keep going, listened as I read excerpts over a shady cell phone connection, and offered thoughtful critiques and suggestions that didn't occur to my Leo self. You are a precious gem, beautiful Capricorn lady, and I appreciate your wise counsel. May the future hold too many moments of laughter to count as we journey the Goddess road together!

I strive always to walk through life with an open heart, to learn, and to be and do better. To the supportive and generous people who helped me navigate my journey to evolve this book with more accurate and inclusive language, thank you for answering my near-endless questions, for the gentle corrections, and for your thoughtfulness and wisdom. I see you, and I honor your journey. I hope you find your wonderful advice is reflected, at least somewhat, in these pages.

To Judika Illes, editor extraordinaire and beloved friend, thank you is not enough. Your kind words and gentle but firm manner of encouragement were so helpful as I struggled to birth this book into being. I appreciate you, and your immense talent, so very much.

To all at Weiser who contributed to this book's publication, thank you. Your skill and professionalism are stellar.

To the genealogists from whom I've sought advice and opinions, thank you for your wisdom and for not batting an eyelash when I mentioned the premise of this book. I hope I have shown that the science of genealogy can blend well with the intangible nature of magic.

To those who feel set apart from genealogy: You and your truths are necessary to maintain the integrity and authenticity of humanity's weaving. As you walk this path of magic, please know that you are seen and valued.

Our guidance sometimes comes from those of whom we are unaware. Over many years, long before I knew of her, the ancient genealogist Hyndla inspired me to gently weave my fingers into the great ancestral web so that I might find my truths. I am filled with gratitude.

Lastly, I pray my words are worthy enough to serve as an homage to the memory of my ancestors. I am me, thanks to them, and I am so grateful for the luck of the genetic draw that gifted me with an insatiable curiosity about the past. I am humbled and honored to carry them with me as I walk this path of magic.

Author Bio

Cairelle Crow has walked a goddess path for more than thirty years, exploring, learning, and growing. She has been involved in genealogical pursuits since the late 1990s and began to actively work with genetic genealogy in 2013. She is the owner of Sacred Roots, which is dedicated to connecting all people to their ancestral heritage, and she lectures locally, nationally, and internationally on the blending of genealogy with magic. She is cofoundress of the Sanctuary of Brigid and its flame-keeping circle, Sisters of the Flame, and is coeditor of the anthology *Brigid's Light* (Weiser, 2022). She is also a holistic RN and co-owner of The Maven Collective, which facilitates sacred experiences for magical women of a certain age. When she's not roaming the world in search of grandmothers and stone circles, Cairelle is home in New Orleans, where she lives joyfully, loves intensely, and laughs frequently with beloved family and friends. You can find her online at *www.cairellecrow.com*, *www.sacredrootsgen.com*, and *www.themavencollective.com*.

To Our Readers

Weiser Books, an imprint of Red Wheel/Weiser, publishes books across the entire spectrum of occult, esoteric, speculative, and New Age subjects. Our mission is to publish quality books that will make a difference in people's lives without advocating any one particular path or field of study. We value the integrity, originality, and depth of knowledge of our authors.

Our readers are our most important resource, and we appreciate your input, suggestions, and ideas about what you would like to see published.

Visit our website at *www.redwheelweiser.com*, where you can learn about our upcoming books and free downloads, and also find links to sign up for our newsletter and exclusive offers.

You can also contact us at *info@rwwbooks.com* or at

Red Wheel/Weiser, LLC

65 Parker Street, Suite 7

Newburyport, MA 01950